"I know Lee Brown as a ~~student~~ distinguished himself as a ~~student and has~~ taken that same approach to ministry. Lee has written a book that is both a labor of love for others to know the fullness of following Jesus, as well as the result of his deep love in following Jesus for himself. I encourage you to read and apply what you find in these pages, you will be the better for it."

—Dr. Cliff Sanders, Chair of Biblical Studies,
Mid-America Christian University

"What a great book to encourage believers of any age and stage in life. I feel encouraged, and am truly glad I took the time to read this. It was inspiring and informative."

—Matt Baird, Lead Singer for heavy metal band Spoken

"Lee Brown is an honest and experienced writer, gifted in far more than just the casual writing style found among his peers. I would have to say that his contributions and writings for my website, IndieVisionMusic, have been crucial towards expanding our fan and readership base at a global level. The talent of this one writer is something I am most impressed with and would recommend this book to anyone seeking truth in a broken world."

—Brandon Jones, Founder and Owner, IndieVisionMusic.com

"Lee is a young, intelligent, and enthusiastic leader. His passion for spiritual growth is evident in his writing. He is a key leader in the church of the future."

—Marty Grubbs, Senior Pastor, Crossings Community Church

"This book is an excellent resource for practical help in making disciples in obedience to the Great Commission."

—Dr. Wendell Sutton, Professor of Theology,
Mid-America Christian University

"Great information. Must read!"

"In Matthew 28, we learn that as Christians we must be disciples of Christ and pour our lives into others. If you are looking to take your walk with Christ to the next level, discipleship is the key. 'Here's How: An Introduction to Practical Discipleship' by Lee Brown is a great guide and tool to use for discovering what true discipleship is. No matter where you are at in your walk with Christ, this book will help you strive to follow Christ and serve Him at a new and deeper level. True discipleship is a life changing experience and through us God wants to change the world! Learn more about what being a disciple of Christ truly looks like and start a life changing journey today!"

HERE'S HOW

LEE BROWN

Portions of Making Sense Out Of Spirituality by Dr. Cliff Sanders used by permission of the author.

Discipleship material originally created by Dr. Charles Lake used by permission of the author.

01/11/13 interview with Brian "Head" Welch used by permission
of Brian "Head" Welch and IndieVisionMusic.com.

Illustrations accredited to Steve Seaton used by permission.

Cover Artwork by Matt Frush.

WestBow Press books may be ordered through booksellers or by contacting:

WestBow Press
A Division of Thomas Nelson
1663 Liberty Drive
Bloomington, IN 47403
www.westbowpress.com
1-(866) 928-1240

ISBN: 978-1-4497-9459-0 (sc)
ISBN: 978-1-4497-9458-3 (hc)
ISBN: 978-1-4497-9460-6 (e)

Library of Congress Control Number: 2013908540

Printed in the United States of America.

WestBow Press rev. date: 6/10/2013

Table of Contents

ACKNOWLEDGEMENTS vii

PREFACE xi

INTRODUCTION PART 1—INTRODUCTION TO DISCIPLESHIP xv

INTRODUCTION PART 2—JUST WHAT IS A DISCIPLESHIP
GROUP? xxiii

LESSON 1—THE DISCIPLINED CHRISTIAN 1

LESSON 2—BUILDING A FIRM FOUNDATION 12

LESSON 3—MEANINGFUL MOMENTS WITH THE MASTER............ 30

LESSON 4—HIDING GOD'S WORD 47

LESSON 5—MY RELATIONSHIP WITH CHRIST 57

LESSON 6—COMMUNICATION WITH YOUR BEST FRIEND 71

LESSON 7—DEALING WITH TEMPTATION 85

LESSON 8—THE MINISTRY OF THE HELPER 97

LESSON 9—COMMITTING TO CHRIST'S BODY............................ 107

LESSON 10—MY ROLE IN THE KINGDOM 128

LESSON 11—WHO IS LORD, ANYWAY? 139

LESSON 12—GO! 159

DISCIPLE COMMISSIONING 173

AFTERWARD.. 175

BIBLE MEMORY SHEET 179

QUIET TIME LOG 181

Acknowledgements—

I once read that it takes a village to get a book into a "final" product. The backbone of the material presented here is the work of Dr. Charles Lake, who has spent decades working to further the cause of discipleship. Steve Seaton first presented the work to me by walking me through a time of interpersonal discipleship. As professor of Evangelism and Discipleship at Mid-America Christian University at the time, Steve met with and discipled a group of aspiring pastors in the little free time he had.

Dr. Cliff Sanders is responsible for lighting a fire under me (and countless others) when it comes to understanding not only what I believe about God…but why. Cliff taught me how to read the Bible in a real and powerful way. He also taught me how to preach Biblically. But perhaps the greatest gift Dr. Sanders ever gave me was the idea that until you understand who you really believe God is, deep down, nothing else in your theology matters. Chapter two of this work is based upon Cliff's extensive work in this area. I cannot more highly recommend his own writing, *Making Sense Out of Spirituality*.

To complete the "Triumvirate of S's," it was Dr. Wendell Sutton who worked with me through the joys of several systematic and practical theology classes. Without him, the last lesson in this discipleship material would be sorely missing. Wendell also gave me my first opportunity to try my hand at being a college professor. For that and so much more, I am forever grateful.

I am also eternally grateful to Shea Moore, Dr. Sutton's daughter, for taking on the painstaking task of editing the work and preparing it for publication. Without her, distracting mechanical and grammatical issues would certainly abound. I should note that she didn't get a chance to edit this paragraph, so any potential errors in it and other areas I "tinkered with" are resoundingly my own.

Danny Jackson, a dear friend, helped me continue to shape and edit the discipleship program used at Branches Student Ministries that ultimately produced this work. His contributions and ideas (notably the idea to put your memory verse on the wall opposite the toilet...practical stuff) shaped the course of at least two revisions to this material.

Of course, it was my buddy, David Lake, who first got me going to church. My youth pastor, Joe Ganahl, who invited me to accept a calling to ministry. It was my family who supported me when I set out into the world with a vision to change it, but no idea how. Who knew trying to become a Professional Wrestler for Jesus would lead me here? Shawn Lovett helped me decide whether I should return to college. Shawn, Rob Grams, Justin Brown, Kyle Garen, Travis Blankenship, Mike Normand, and a handful of others helped me make Smallville night a tradition that lasted long past college. My wife, Renae, who has inspired me to become a better man, and my son Logan who brings new joy to my life every day and makes me proud that I get to disciple him by sharing my life as his father.

Extra special thanks go out to Jeff and Tacie Dreessen, my family (including my grandparents, Gary and Dolly Wells, mother, Melodi Brown, and step-father, Paul Narloch), my church family at Fresh Start Community Church, and the many others who provided both the inspiration and the financial support that allowed this work to come to fruition.

This is just a part of the village that led to the creation of this work. I pray you and your village will be blessed and challenged forever by it. It's not easy. In fact, Jesus asks for death along the way, but the promise on the other side is LIFE. And it is a life like you never could have imagined.

Lee Brown, April 19, 2013

Preface—

What does it mean to be a disciple? What does that process even look like? If you're like the average follower of Jesus Christ, you've been told to do any number of things in your pursuit of living your life for God. The problem is, though many voices have told you that you should be doing this or that to connect with God, very rarely, if ever, has anyone taken the time to show you how or why.

Perhaps this stems from the fact that, like you, those voices telling us we need to be doing certain things in our walk with God were not properly shown how to do these very things themselves. As "Christians," we've been told many times in our lives that there are certain essential elements to our relationship with God. More likely than not, this charge started and ended in a pulpit or a small group setting, but never went further than that.

Don't get me wrong; as a pastor myself, I would never downplay the role that the exposition of the Word plays in the life of a community of believers. The problem, however, is that for all its merits, preaching is not the primary way that Jesus Christ and His followers learned and taught what it means to follow God, to be like Him, and to change the world.

Discipleship is.

Though Jesus certainly delivered great sermons during His three-year "public ministry," the bulk of what we can see (and have to read between the lines to see) of His ministry was spent pouring Himself into twelve men and telling them that the fate of His message would soon rest in their hands.

Apparently, it worked. You and I and everyone else who have ever claimed that Jesus is the Messiah can trace our coming to know God through the work of eleven of the twelve men that Jesus poured His life into and the Apostle Paul, who had a life-changing meeting with Jesus while walking down the road of life. Discipleship was always the plan God had to change the world. Indeed, it still is.

In this work, you'll find the bare bones of what it means to move from being a "Christian" to becoming a disciple of Jesus the Christ. This goes much deeper than simple information on a page. This is truly a process of life transformation. While you'll encounter some great information, if you don't allow it to travel the great distance from your head to your heart and finally to your hands, you have not truly undertaken the process that Jesus Himself modeled. Not even a little bit.

Because of this, you'll see various assignments with each "lesson." These are not meant to give you homework for no good reason, but rather to initiate the process by which you can know what it means to pray, memorize Scripture, and commune with the Living God. The book you're holding is not simply meant for reading. It's a process screaming out for you to undertake it and live it out with a small group of fellow warriors seeking to be molded after the heart of their King. Wherever you are in your walk with Christ, it's time to begin a process that moves us from being sedentary "Christians" to becoming disciples of the Only Son of God.

This process was, is, and always will be best lived out through sharing life with others. Therefore, I recommend taking others along with you for the journey and forming a discipleship group. Jesus started with twelve. It doesn't take a mob to change the world.

If you've never been through interpersonal discipleship in the past, I suggest finding a follower of Christ who has taken others through a discipleship process and asking them to work with you through this material. At the very least, I recommend having someone (a pastor, a leader in your church, a trusted and aged follower of Christ) who will be there for you as you enter this process. Know this: the process comes alive when it is struggled through with others.

If you're further along in your walk with God, I challenge you to look at this material through fresh eyes. Don't fall into the trap of coming to the Scriptures and the lessons with preconceived notions. See it as if you were seeing it for the first time. Often, what we think we know can become a hindrance to allowing further truths to make a dent in our thick heads. It can be like an inoculation that allows the little bit we have to prevent us from getting infected with the real deal.

Get ready for life change. Get ready to learn both *how* and *why* to take an active role in the disciplines that Christians throughout time have associated with a strong walk with the Lord. Get ready to begin. And begin is truly the word here. This work is not the end-all of discipleship. It is simply the starting blocks. Discipleship is a lifelong process that finds its completion only when we stand before a Holy God. What you're about to enter into is a set of processes, a group of tools that will allow you to stand before that God knowing that you've walked by His side and led others to do the same.

Go. Make Disciples.

Introduction Part 1—
Introduction to Discipleship

Over a decade after becoming a Christian, I sat in my first college class dedicated to eventually turning me into a pastor. This was *the* class to be in. Students all around campus rumbled and murmured about the bold testimonies older students shared with them of what was in store for us in "Biblical Life and Witness." Many seniors opted to take this class again in their free time before they left the university...even without getting any further credit for it. It was also one of only a handful of classes taught by the Chair of the whole Ministry Department.[1] And it did not disappoint.

I would soon find that this class was marked by deceptively simple truths that ran deep into the faith, and yet, few confront on such an intimate level. To give an example, early on in the semester Dr. Sanders asked the class a simple question that penetrated through the preconceived notions I had already built up in my mind about what it meant to "follow God."

"Who has been told that they *should* read the Bible?" Dr. Sanders asked in his usual straightforward manner. In a class of about eighty college freshmen, many of whom were studying to go into a life in the ministry, every single hand raised with a quiet uproar. With a

---

[1]   Dr. Sanders is that sort of professor that made hardened criminals tremble. Just ask him about his time with the Banditos.

smirk, Cliff slowly added, "How many of you have ever really and truly been shown *how* to read the Bible?"

As I thought seriously about the question, my hand began to quickly descend. A small wave of self-doubt came over me as I dropped it back down to my lap. I was not alone. Across the room, seventy-plus hands rapidly went back down, leaving only a small number still raised. As my eyes darted across the room, a sudden realization came upon me. I was sitting in a Christian university, surrounded by nearly a hundred individuals, who have very likely spent quite a bit of time in church sitting through countless sermons, Sunday School classes, and church gatherings, and yet we as a collective mass had never made it past the fact that we should be doing some certain things and not doing others. In a room full of future pastors, only a few had been shown the how and the deeper why behind it all.

Now don't get me wrong; I learned quite a bit from my church and I certainly had things together to some degree. Still, the striking fact that so many hands went down in an instant told me something I was afraid to hear. On average in the life of the church today, people are told over and over again that they should pray, they should read their Bible, they should take care of the poor, and that they should get to know God as their ultimate relationship, but very few are ever taken there, one on one, by someone who is doing it themselves.

What I'm talking about goes so much deeper than simply listening to a sermon series on spending time with God. It goes deeper than a small group setting where a gaggle of friends get together and try to study the Bible. What I'm talking about is apprenticeship. I'm talking about getting down in the trenches with another soul and showing them through long hours together what it looks like practically to do these basic things we tell people should be a part of every Christian's life. I'm talking about getting to the point where we could confidently lead others through this great journey. I'm talking about what could happen when someone like you catches that fire and starts to show others what it's all about. Discipleship isn't simple addition; it's all about compound multiplication.[2]

The sad thing is that, on the average, this simply isn't happening in the lives of the very people who call themselves "followers" of Jesus Christ. To our discredit, we rely only on sermons[3], rather than a deep level of life transference and face-to-face interaction. Even when we do get face-to-face, we all begin from the same level of ignorance. This is not a harsh knock against any believers in particular. The sad fact is that if we have not been trained on the how's and why's, then we *are* in a position of ignorance.

Again, let me be clear; these are all greatly important in adding to our walk with God, but they don't replace discipleship. This is especially true when no discipleship has taken place to begin with. We see in the Scriptures in Luke 4:16 that Jesus "made it a regular practice" to attend what has evolved into our modern worship service, yet the bulk of His ministry was spent on a daily grind with the twelve men we now call Apostles...or disciples. Jesus didn't just go to church; He took the Church with Him. Discipleship was a common practice in the Jewish world of His day, and for good reason.

To some degree, we still do this in modern society—just not always in the church. We call these people journeymen, interns, understudies, and even apprentices. In some professions, the preferred mode of training is still that deep on-the-job interaction where someone who has been there will take someone coming into

---

[2] This is the most you'll ever hear me talk about mathematics. The calculator app on my phone probably gets more use than any other app!

[3] Here's a fun game. Try to count the number of sermons you've heard in your life. Now subtract the ones you slept through...even if you just dosed off for a minute. (Note: I'm sorry for going back on what I just said and asking you to do a math problem. It won't happen again. This time I REAALLYY promise.)

the trade and show them the ropes. Life transference happens best in that setting. It just doesn't happen that way, on average, in our "holy" meetings. We've moved to the entertainment model, instead, where we focus on what "*I* can get out of the experience."

It seems as if the average Christian today truly believes that if they attend service a handful of times in a year, pick up their Bible every once in a while, and say a quick prayer before every meal that they are following the plan Jesus had for His people. That's not how it's supposed to be.

As with the answer to so many rhetorical Sunday school questions[4], the life of Jesus the Christ is our model to find what it means to give our life to God and to begin to receive new life from Him. 2 Corinthians 5:17 says that anyone who has done this is now a new creation through Christ. It tells us that the old ways have passed from us and that a new creation is born. Yet, too many of us have nothing more to our "new" life than a sudden awareness that we should probably stop smoking and maybe delete a few inappropriate pictures from our Facebook page.

Jesus' life shows us something so much more radical. Jesus, Who was and is God in the flesh, spent a majority of His time making a small group of men into His personal apprentices. He showed them what to do, taught them how, and reminded them of why this whole thing was important. Several times in the Gospels you'll see Jesus remind this ragtag group that pretty soon He'll be gone and everything will be up to them. Pay attention, because this is exactly what Jesus is saying to us. In fact, they were His very last audible words.

We give a lot of attention to what people's "last words" are. History books are replete with great generals', emperors', and heroes'

---

[4]   Jesus is always the answer in Sunday school. Sorry for giving that secret away. At least you'll have the answer ready when they try to spring questions on you while you're thinking about the 1970's forest green suit the Sunday school teacher is wearing that day.

final utterances before they passed from this life. We somehow know that these words are of great importance. The most significant final words came from a resurrected Jesus telling His followers to go into the entire world and make disciples. Basically, He told this group to go and live like He showed them to live. He took the training wheels off and gave them that last little push.

If those were the final words from the very Son of God, shouldn't we pay close attention to them? I won't insult you to say that we don't all try to some degree. The fact that you're reading this book tells me that you're honestly trying to know how to make Christ's last words a bigger part of your life. It's just that so many of us forget that what Jesus asked of His followers was complete and utter surrender. He even said radical things like, "die to yourself daily" (Luke 9:23). There certainly is a little bit of the extreme needed in true and honest discipleship.

So let's come to the point. This introduction asks two main things of you that will set the tone for the rest of this book. First, it asks that you get serious. Discipleship is not something you add on to your present walk with God as just another to-do list item. It's not a New Year's Resolution you make in January and give up on in January-and-a-half. It's more like demolishing your whole pattern of life to the ground and rebuilding it from the ground up.

In the course of this material, you'll find that we must go back to the basics on many things and construct a fresh foundation for your Christian walk. That's a bit intense, I would say, but as you'll come to see, Jesus asked extreme things of His disciples to get them to where He wanted to take them. He was pretty serious about that taking up your cross and following Him thing.

To this end, you'll be asked to make certain commitments through the rest of this book. These commitments include daily time with God in His Word and in prayer, keeping a Quiet Time Log of your time spent with God, and memorization of one to two Scriptures per week. Additionally, it's imperative that you open your life up to the accountability of another believer or small group of fellow disciples. Most of all, this process demands that you begin to reorient and retrain many of your formerly unhealthy habits into ones that are more directly informed by the life of Jesus the Messiah.

The second thing this introduction asks you to do is to set aside what you think you already know. Because discipleship is often left off of the Spiritual "buffet" we treat our walk with God like, I ask that you come to this material with fresh eyes. Whether you've just become a follower of Jesus Christ or you're a fellow pastor looking for something to bring back some spiritual zest, I ask you to look at each section as though it were brand new to you. Meditate on it. Ask God what He thinks. Test it against His Word. This is what we are called to do, after all, with any message we receive[5].

Only after you've done this can you truly begin to rebuild on a fresh foundation. I'm not saying throw out everything you know about God. I'm saying allow this process to shape and reshape the foundation upon which you have built your spiritual house. After you've reformed that foundation, then you may begin to rebuild your spiritual house back into proper order. I promise you'll like what you can build on a solid foundation much more than a cracked and broken one.

Discipleship is about life change. That life change begins now. In the following chapter, we're going address what discipleship is and is not, and then we'll begin to walk through that process. The chapters that follow will ask you to spend one week marinating in both the informative and transformative processes being taught. All said and done, I'm asking you to commit to twelve weeks. Twelve

---

5   Well, some people don't want you to test what they have to say against what God says. Those people are called _____. (Aren't fill-in-the-blanks fun?)

weeks to demolish and rebuild a spiritual foundation upon the rock of Christ that will withstand to the end.

This process would best be done in a group of five to ten disciples with someone who has walked the path ahead. It would be ideal for the group to meet formally for about an hour and a half to two hours on a recurring day of the week to go through the material and its impact on your thinking and your doing. In addition to this, the group should pair up and encourage each other throughout the week to continue walking the path, working through the lessons, and doing the required tasks. As Dr. Sanders says, we don't often do what is expected, we do what is inspected.

If working through this process with others is somehow just not possible for you, don't give up. I still encourage you to work through the material and pray that God would provide a group of passionate disciples to join alongside your journey. Remember, discipleship is how the Son of the Living God chose to put His Gospel in our hands. Jesus didn't invest in a fifty-fifty option. He put everything, the entire power of His life, into the hands of a group that we still call today...the disciples.

What is a disciple? You're about to be one. Welcome to the journey.

Introduction Part 2—
Just What Is a Discipleship Group?

Perhaps the single most common reason discipleship doesn't happen as it should is that we've replaced the deep systematic process of life transference with a more routine time of meeting in a small group just to chat. As important as fellowship is in the life of the church, this is not discipleship. Discipleship is not something that you simply add to your plate in order to prove to yourself and others that you're "the real deal." Discipleship, as Rev. Steve Seaton points out, is about a new life in Christ. However, this new life means that we must also develop new life-styles. Discipleship involves a new way of living based on daily time with God and application of His Word.

So, while I'm certainly not encouraging the church to stop fellowshipping[6], discipleship is something inherently more intentional. It means that you're learning to feed yourself from God's Word and apply it to your own life rather than merely relying on someone else to come up with three points a week from some verse in the Bible we may or may not have read and likely only saw for a couple of seconds on a PowerPoint slide.

---

[6] Some of our best chances to eat come in the form of "fellowship." So much so, in fact, that despite long hours trying to find the answer in my Bible, I still haven't figured out how the disciples were able to fellowship before Red Robin Burgers were invented.

To clarify, let me give you two categorical things that discipleship is not. First of all, true discipleship groups are not a Bible study. Don't misunderstand me to think I just said that you're not studying the Bible. A real discipleship group, however, is not simply reading with some friends through Revelation and then asking what everyone in the room thinks it might mean[7]. Dr. Charles Lake puts it more bluntly, "Discipleship is not a Bible study. It is an attempt to establish Biblical disciplines to ensure the growth and maturity of every believer in relationship with Christ[8]."

You may still be confused as to what the difference is. In a typical Bible study, persons meet and discuss a small portion of the Bible, all the while asking each other what insights they got from it, and what they think it means. While this is an amazing practice that you will definitely need back in your spiritual house in its time, this is not what we're asking of you here. What we're asking, as Dr. Lake mentions, is to establish Biblical disciplines that will serve as a framework through which your Bible study, prayer, and other means of grace will naturally flow. In many ways, we're asking you to reconstruct your worldview through the lens of a process Jesus handed down to His followers.

Secondly, a discipleship group should not be confused with the function of a fellowship group. Think of discipleship in terms of your job. If we were to compare the two, a fellowship group would be closest to what you do in the break room. This is the place where you meet and share your concerns with one another. Fellowship groups (also called prayer groups, small groups, life groups, etc.) often spend much of their time asking each member how their week has been, what exciting new things are going on, and, of course, where God is working in their lives.

---

[7]   Which, of course, is another fun game in and of itself.

[8]   Lake, Charles. *Discipleship Training: A Venture in Learning and Accountability*, Growth Ministries: Greenwood, revised edition, 1992.

Such groups are indispensible to the life of the Church, but they are not discipleship groups. Discipleship groups are meant to be a purposeful time used to cover specific aspects of our lives in relation to our growth in Christ and not simply time to update each other on what's going on in our lives. I'm not saying that this cannot ever make its way into your discipleship group time, however. Occasionally, an event will happen and compassion and sharing will need to overshadow a disciplined regime for a short time. However, the average discipleship setting is a time where those involved come focused and ready to go to the places that God is taking them.

Those are two broad categories of what a discipleship group is not. So what is a discipleship group, then? Discipleship groups have at least six elements. First of all, a discipleship group is a weekly time of training and accountability. Each week the discipleship group has an element of direct training that is to be applied in the life of the disciple. Similar to a sermon in some ways, it is information that leads to transformation. Except, in contrast to a sermon, this would be like having the pastor sit down with you and work through your questions and thoughts along the way. Rather than the one on anywhere from fifty to 1,000,000 dynamic of a sermon, this is more contained to one or two disciple-makers to every ten or so learners.

Secondly, a discipleship group is about application. In *The Slumber of Christianity*, author Ted Dekker wrote, "Christians aren't really so different from non-Christians, certainly not on the scale you would expect considering the promises of love, joy, and peace boldly pronounced from thousands of pulpits across the land. We spend our money on the same kinds of entertainment, we buy the same kinds of foods and clothes, and we spend as much time searching for purpose.[9]" While Dekker's assertion is based on the fact that

---

[9]   Dekker, Ted. *The Slumber of Christianity*, Thomas Nelson: Nashville, 2005, 9.

Christians have lost the joy and promise of heaven from their hearts, his words still echo true to what we are talking about here.

Though application of God's Word should be a common element in sermons, Bible study, prayer groups, and fellowship groups alike, discipleship groups are much more intensely purposeful about ensuring the disciple has begun the hard process of not just hearing, but doing. As Rev. Steve Seaton says, "Discipleship training focuses on application of Biblical principles to daily living." In many ways, it's a difference of intensity and intentionality.

Third, a discipleship group is a time for prayer and partnership. This may seem confusing or contradictory to what was said above. Remember, this is not a time to share every little thing that's going on in your life. However, discipleship does involve opening up your life to a group of fellow disciples. Though it should not dominate the time when you are meeting for the lesson, discipleship groups do give a time to learn what prayer together really is and put that into action. In addition to this, you are asked to spend some time outside of the "lesson time" in which you will meet (phone, in person, etc.[10]) with another member or members from the group to pray and encourage one another.

Fourth, a discipleship group carries with it the element of accountability. Too many people who consider themselves "spiritual giants[11]" leave this all-important element out of their walk with Christ. As unfortunate as it is, our default mode since the Fall has been sin. Yes, as we have seen, we are a new creation in Christ and new attitudes were enabled in us when we gave our life over to Him, but we're still susceptible to temptations to sin. If that were not the case, you would never hear of pastors cheating on their wives with

---

[10]   Skype, Oovoo, FaceTime, Google+, even Facebook…there are just so many things that eliminate excuses in this area in today's day and age.

[11]   Not to be confused with Andre the Giant, star of *the Princess Bride* and Wrestlemania 3.

their secretary[12]. You would never hear of that once-great person you looked up to who ruined his/her life due to a secret addiction. The fact is, as Pastor Dave Dooley says, "it" (whatever "it" is) can still happen to you.

In teaching on this topic during a chapel service at Mid-America Christian University, Pastor Dooley began with a clip from the movie *Bambi*. In the film, Bambi, Thumper, and friends are being taught about becoming "twitterpated[13]," and the bulk of the scene has the wise old owl going one by one, pointing them out and repeating, "It can happen to you...it can happen to you," that is, until the owl's finger lands on the skunk, in which the exclamation is made, "Well...maybe not to you!"

The sad fact is we are not skunks in this scenario (and for once that's a bad thing). "It" can and will happen to us if we don't have a plan in place. Dr. Cliff Sanders teaches that "People do not do what is expected; they do what is inspected," in life. That is to say, the average person like you or I often times will not do _____ [14]because it is expected of us, but because someone will be checking up on us later. This is something that we must work on lessening through God's work in our lives. Accountability becomes the best way to help one another stay on task.

Each week of this program you're asked to meet with your accountability partner(s) and ask each other hard questions about whether or not you've read the required reading, memorized the Scripture word perfect, and spent time in prayer and reading from

---

[12] Ironically, pastors are humans, too. For some reason when I was little I thought they were special creations born without fault. Then I became one and ruined that mold. Turns out, we have struggles, too. This is also why all pastors should require their personal secretary be at least 80.

[13] Which, it turns out, has nothing to do with Twitter. Since, you know, the movie was released August 21, 1942.

[14] More fun with fill-in-the-blanks!

God's Word. It may sound phony to have someone checking up on you, but I promise you'll appreciate the drive that comes from knowing someone is actually going to call you on your junk. It should be pointed out, of course, that you will need to muster the courage to be direct and honest with each other, confronting each other in love about what you are and are not doing to further your walk with God. This is a key element of the process.

Fifth, comes the element of Scripture memorization. For the twelve weeks I'm asking you to commit to, these verses have been preselected and are to be read and memorized from the versions included. The reason for this is that we want everyone in the discipleship group to be on the same page. This is, in Steve Seaton's words, "systematic, regular Scripture memorization and meditation." Though I will elaborate on this in a later section, it is important to know that for this course, we will memorize these in a particular way, as well.

When memorizing Scripture for this course, you will begin and end with the verse reference. For example, the first week's verse is 2 Corinthians 5:17. You would memorize it as: "2 Corinthians 5:17, Therefore, if anyone is in Christ, he is a new creation. The old has passed away; behold the new has come. 2 Corinthians 5:17." The reason we learn the verse reference as a part of the whole and place it at the start and at the end of the verse is that too many people (myself included) know quite a bit of Scripture and couldn't tell you in a week where to find it.

To quote another memory verse coming up, this is all about "storing up" God's Word in our hearts. If it is truly to be stored in our hearts, we ask that it have the verse reference with it (and followed by it) and that it is *word perfect*. What this means is that as you spend time in your discipleship group reciting the verses, you make sure that your own recitation and that of the person you're paired up with is exactly word for word.

You may feel a bit overwhelmed by this task, but know that many of the verses are extremely short and to the point. There are only a few that are a bit longer. For those, you would do well to practice them more often and memorize a few words at a time. Danny Jackson taught me the practice of hanging a copy of the memory verses across from where I sit when I have to go to the bathroom. This way, I know at least once a day I will see the verses and have some time to recite them. That may sound crude, but going before the Throne of God from the porcelain throne is a very helpful tool I've used in memorizing (or storing up) God's Word in my heart. You may prefer index cards in your pocket. Whatever works best for you.

You'll have accomplished quite a bit when in 12-13 weeks you've got over a dozen Scriptures memorized word perfect and hidden in your heart. We'll talk in a few lessons about how to do this and why it is important. But, just know that from the very first week, you are asked to meditate upon and learn a portion of Scripture.

Lastly, the discipleship group is a place for support and mutual uplifting. You should be meeting with a group of concerned, encouraging, fellow disciples. You should begin to develop a true sense of community as you go. That said, though it should not nudge out the other elements by demanding more time, there is certainly a place before, after, and sometimes during, to share where you are in life and where God is taking you. You should be able to go to these fellow disciples and share in your struggles, feeling confident that this will not be misused. These should be fellow warriors fighting fiercely alongside you against the enemy of your soul.

When it comes down to it, the Christian life is active, not passive. Discipleship involves moving from complacency to commitment and from inactivity to involvement. It is a bit extreme at times, but it's meant to be. It can be tough, but I wouldn't have it any other way. So, before we move into the course material itself, allow me to give you what I expect from my discipleship group whenever we go through this material, as well as a commitment sheet that I use to encourage and remind the disciples of the journey about to be traveled.

Requirements

1. Perfect attendance, except in the event of unavoidable absences related to work, illness, or serious emergency. It is strongly suggested that you do your best not to miss more than twice. You may contact your disciple-maker to make up sessions missed.
2. Memorization of weekly Scripture passages is required.
3. Submission of a Quiet Time Log for each week of the twelve-week course.
4. An honest attempt to pray weekly with your prayer partner.
5. To strive to lead others into a discipleship process and thereby further the Great Commission.

My Discipleship Commitment

To the best of my ability, I hereby commit myself to this phase of Discipleship training. I will do my best to faithfully attend each session and wholeheartedly attempt to apply the daily disciplines I am taught within the journey.

_____   _____

Signature of Disciple   Signature of Disciple-maker

"Everyone to whom much is given, of him much will be required, and from him to whom they entrusted much, they will demand the more" (ESV).
Luke 12:48

Lesson 1—

The Disciplined Christian

Quick question: How many Bibles do you have in your house? How many Bible apps could you download to your phone or tablet in the next thirty seconds? Though we live in an unprecedented place in history where we are freely able to own a Bible for ourselves (let alone read it freely and openly without fear of persecution and death), we as followers of Christ simply do not. As with the revelation I had in the "Biblical Life and Witness" class I mentioned in the opening of this book, it has been hammered into our heads from pulpits across the globe every week that we should read the Bible. Yet, we simply don't.

Or, maybe we tried here or there, but it seemed distant and uninteresting, too hard to understand, and not really able to be applied to our lives. Or, more than likely, as followers of Christ we see the need to read our Bibles, but simply fall into a habit where we just don't do it much. Maybe your Bible sits on your dresser beside your bed, in your backpack in your locker, or perhaps you already have an app on your phone for it, but no matter where it is, it doesn't get opened much.

You know you should.

You sometimes just forget.

You don't see why it's all that important.

You don't really know where to begin.

It's for this very reason that the first lesson in your process of discipleship may seem the least spiritual of them all. We're going to have to talk about discipline. This assumes that you understand that the Bible is relevant and important for your life and that God desires for us to meet Him there daily. If you don't understand this, however, give me just a brief moment to explain why. We will also come back to this in a later lesson. It's important that you understand that the Bible is the very Word of God. Whatever you believe about how we got it and what version is the best, almost all Christians can agree that the Bible is the Living Word of the Living God.

To further this, Hebrews 4:12 points out that this book we hold has power. It is living and active and sharper than any two edged sword. This book is the only book in the history of the world that has remained absolutely relevant to every moment in the history of the world. It is the very Word that God gave us as a manual for our own lives, as well as a history of His redemption story. The Bible is also the most widely circulated, widely read, and widely referenced work of literature in the history of the world. No matter what you believe about the inspiration of the Bible, it is nearly impossible to intelligently downplay its importance.

So, the reason we don't start with a theological lesson is that often our problem in coming before the Throne of God is not a lack of understanding of its importance, but a lack of discipline. Discipline is a dirty word in our culture today. It sounds like something an old drill sergeant would expect of a regiment of troops...and honestly, that's not far from the truth. But, just because discipline is unpopular in our culture, doesn't mean we're excused from the requirement it places on our lives.

Dr. Jay Adams, in his article *Godliness through Discipline*, notes that, "Today we have instant pudding, instant coffee, instant houses shipped on trucks, instant everything. And we want instant godliness as well. We want somebody to give us three easy steps to godliness, and we'll take them next Friday and be godly. The trouble is, godliness doesn't come about that way." He then adds, "Discipline *is* the path to godliness[15]."

In his letter to a young leader named Timothy, Paul states, you must "discipline yourself for the purpose of godliness.[16]" He doesn't give us an option here. Paul says that discipline is a must. Does it surprise you then that discipline and disciple both come from the same root word? Or, would it surprise you to learn that their root word gives us the image of an athlete in training? It shouldn't.

Regardless of the fact that discipline is out of style in the world today, the truth remains that there is no other path to becoming like Christ than through discipline. Take a look through the pages of the Bible and you'll see Paul and Jesus alike tooting on this same horn. The message is loud and clear that without discipline, we will not become what Christ has asked of us. We will never become the living sacrifice we were meant to be if we do not subject ourselves to sit under the tutelage of discipline. There is no godliness without discipline.

Though I would love to start the path to your discipleship with the foundation we will destroy and rebuild in the next lesson, the shocking fact remains that if we do not first get into a framework of discipline, the remainder of our efforts will become increasingly fruitless. Worst of all, if we do not take captive our bodies and minds to this end, we run the risk of limping our way through our discipleship while assuming we're running a marathon.

Why is discipline important? Without it, you will not look much like Christ. Worse still, you may somehow actually convince yourself that you do anyway. From that point, you may even convince yourself that you need nothing further or that you have been there and done that. As I said, this is the framework (not to be confused with the

---

[15]   Adams, Jay. *Godliness Through Discipline,* P & R Publishing: Phillipsburg, second edition. 1983.

[16]   1 Timothy 4:7

foundation) that we must erect if we are to start down the path of true discipleship.

Deepening discipleship begins, says Dr. Charles Lake, with the realization that along with a new life in Christ[17], a new lifestyle must be developed. It would be nice if this would happen the instant we accept Christ, but that is not the case. The truth is, there is no instant maturity. Spiritual discipline is the key to spiritual maturity. Discipline is the key. Repeat that out loud and think about the implications of it.

In the most basic form, our discipline comes down to what we allow to become our habits. Dr. Jay Adams has said, "God has given us an amazing capacity we call habit. We may use that capacity for good or evil. Surrendered to the Lord, we can pattern our lives towards growth and maturity[18]." In essence, habit is a tool we use daily that shapes our lives. Think about it. How much of what you do is done out of habit? Have you ever found yourself incredibly frustrated when your "usual" route to a certain place is under construction or there's a wreck that causes you to have to go a different way? Typically, it doesn't take you any thought at all to get from Point A to Point B, and you can see that even more clearly when this pattern is disrupted. It has simply become habit.

Do you brush your teeth side-to-side or top to bottom? Which direction do you hang your toilet paper, overhand or underhand?[19] When you get up, what's the first thing you do every morning? When you get into the shower, what do you always scrub first? As you can see, human beings are creatures of habit. We were designed by God to be that way. This is neither sinful nor holy in and of itself, but make no mistake, your habits are either trained to be the

---

[17] 2 Corinthians 5:17

[18] Ibid.

[19] Always overhand. Just in case you care.

4

very force that moves you on in your relationship with God, or your spiritual destruction.

"I am your constant companion. I am your greatest helper or heaviest burden. I will push you onward or drag you down to failure. I am completely at your command. Half the things you do you might as well turn over to me and I will be able to do them quickly and correctly. I am easily managed—You must merely be firm with me. Show me exactly how you want something done and after a few lessons I will do it automatically. I am the servant of all great men; and alas, of all failures, as well. Those who are great, I have made great. Those who are failures, I have made failures. I am not a machine, even though I work with the precision of a machine plus the intelligence of a man. You may run me for profit or you may run me for ruin—it makes no difference to me. Take me, train me, be firm with me, and I will place the world at your feet. Be easy with me and I will destroy you. Who am I? I am habit.[20]"

There's an old Czech proverb that says, "Habit is a shirt made of iron." If you're going to stay the course in becoming a true disciple of the Messiah, you must start by examining your habits. It's said by many that it takes at least three weeks of proper daily effort to feel comfortable in performing a new practice. On top of that, it takes about three more weeks to make the practice a part of oneself. The problem is that, as Dr. Adams said, we want instant discipleship. We want to simply hear something that will grow in us like a magic beanstalk and change our lives without any effort. Let me warn you, there is no magic bean[21].

The average Christian doesn't even continue on the path to discipleship for three straight days. Sure, we mean well. We make

---

[20]   This quote is attributed to "anonymous." Despite my best efforts, I just couldn't track "anonymous" down.

[21]   There is, however, beano, which works like magic. Something to think about.

a pact with God that we'll read our Bible and pray, and we really think that we just magically will, but without proper discipline, this well-meaning spirit doesn't produce anything past the initial rush of feelings. And, right there is exactly the problem.

In today's society, we're trained through various ways from a very early age to be slaves to our feelings. The message of our culture is that if it feels right, it must be right. Counter to that, if it doesn't feel the way we want it to, there must be something wrong. This is completely the opposite of what Scripture teaches. Hebrews 12:11 says, "No discipline seems pleasant at the time, but painful. Later on, however, it produces a harvest of righteousness and peace for those who have been trained by it."

The absolute unquestionable truth is that right actions generate right feelings—not the other way around. In your path to discipleship, you may feel uncomfortable having to add such disciplined facets to your faith. It may seem like you're suddenly trying to earn your way to God (which you can't; something we'll discuss in a later lesson). The truth is, though, that no discipline feels good and pleasant to us. Discipline is always uncomfortable—especially at first—but if we continue on and do what we know is right no matter what our feelings tell us to do, a strange thing happens. After a while, our doing the right actions will eventually change our feelings around and we'll feel good about it.

It's like working out. I try to get up and work out in the mornings. This seems, on paper, to work best for my schedule. The problem is, early in the morning I don't feel like getting up. I can immediately rationalize the need for more sleep. But, when I do, I don't get the good benefits I was looking for. Worse, if I get in a habit of missing my work out, then I start to feel really cruddy. Like the true body builder says, "No pain, no gain."

Take a moment and write down on another sheet of paper three areas of your life that show you are a disciplined person. I guarantee you have a few. You are already disciplined to some degree. It could be your routine for your job. Perhaps it is your workout schedule, your diet, or your habits with your kids/parents/spouse. Whatever it is, take a minute and write out three examples.

Now, take a moment to write out three areas in which you lack discipline. Everyone has them. It may even be the other side of the examples given above. Maybe you're struggling with your diet. Perhaps you don't have good family habits. Whatever they are for you, ponder for a moment and write them down on another piece of paper, in a journal, or in the margins of this page. Use these as discussion points in your discipleship group.

The last area of discipline we're going to talk about is time management. Again, this is not the most spiritual thing we're going to discuss in this course, but it is needed to make the rest of the life transformation happen. If we were to look at our lives in total, all of life's tasks and to-do's can be broken up into four areas or quadrants. See below:

Time Management Grid

	Not Important	Important
Not Urgent	Q1	Q2
Urgent	Q3	Q4

Everything we do in our daily life can be broken down and placed into one of these four quadrants. I want you to look first at the darker shaded boxes. These areas will take care of themselves. By definition, these are tasks that must be done (are important) and done right away (are urgent), so they *will* get done. These are the huge fires we have to put out day to day. Conversely, tasks that are not pressing (not urgent) and have little effect on the course of our future (not important) will automatically be shoved into our mental and spiritual trash bin.

The problem in life comes in the areas that are lighter shaded boxes. Tasks that are urgent, but not important, often crowd out ones that are important, but aren't screaming at you to get them done right now. Discipleship falls into this category. Your Bible will not start ringing until you answer it. God will not come into your office and demand your immediate attention. You will not find your memory verses screaming at you like the kids in the back seat. Our walk with God is incredibly important—indeed, the most important thing there is—but it isn't all that urgent.

It should be, but often we'll find those things that have to be done "right now" will crowd out the God that is always there. The trick in finishing this discipleship course strong (as well as life itself) is found in how you learn to prioritize those tasks that are important over those that are urgent. How do you do this? We'll talk about some tips and tricks in coming lessons that may help, but remember, it all comes down to discipline. It also depends on the extent of your commitment.

Spiritually, those who are uncommitted will not even bother. If you are committed to attending a church, you may try to integrate this into your life just because it is a good practice. If you're committed to being a part of the Body of Christ that "moves" and serves, then you're likely to find the need for discipline much greater. The very fact that you're reading material on discipleship tells me that you're likely already committing yourself to maturity in Christ.

The more committed you desire to become; the more is asked of you. Just as in the Parable of the Talents[22], to whom much is given, much more will be asked. So, be sure you learn to control your habits

---

[22] One of many awesome yet sometimes confusing stories Jesus told to get His points across (Matthew 25:18-30).

and use them as a tool that allows you to grow in Christ to the fullest degree. Speaking of the tools we're using to grow...

Allow me just a moment before we move on to explain the assignments that you'll begin this week and continue through each week to come. I want you to understand what is asked of you. First of all, you're asked to enter into a quiet time with God. What is that? Simply put, this is time with God in the Bible and prayer. Don't know how to start? We'll talk about that in a coming lesson, but for now I always lay out the following guidelines:

1. Start somewhere and move from there

What I mean is that you're not going to be assigned a specific place in the Bible to read. It's up to you to start somewhere. I recommend starting in the Gospels, the Psalms, or Proverbs if you're younger in your faith. Additionally, wherever you start, read the whole book through (this is less pressing in the Proverbs). We'll talk about the reason for this later.

2. Set aside a specific time

Again, you'll see a repeat on this in a later section, but I need you to know that if you "schedule" a regular time with God, you're more likely to actually have that time with Him than if you let the urgent matters in your day crowd this out. This may seem unspiritual, but I assure you, God will show up if you do.

In your daily time of reading, be sure to keep a Quiet Time Log. There is a sample of this in the appendix. Feel free to copy this. Your aim while reading the Bible is to read until you come across something that God is clearly calling to your attention. Find where God is speaking to you. When you find this, write down the verse (or the verse reference) and then answer the following questions on your sheet:

1. What does this mean? (What truth is God's Word teaching in this? NOT, "what do I *think* it is saying," but "what is it *really* saying?" This may require some real study.)
2. What does this mean for my life? (How does the true meaning affect your life?)
3. What am I going to do about it?

This book is about life transformation and application of Scripture. The third question is the part that most people overlook in their faith walk. If you simply read the Scripture and do nothing about it, you're not doing yourself any favors. You must be purposeful in your time with God and allow His Word to change you. Or, to put it in the words of one of the Biblical authors, "Do not merely be hearers of the Word, but doers.[23]"

Next, you'll memorize a selection of Scripture. Remember, you are to memorize it *word perfect* (word for word) from the version selected in this course, as well as beginning and ending the verse with the verse reference. For this week, your verse to learn is 2 Corinthians 5:17.

In addition to this, we'll soon begin to add a prayer partner to the mix, beginning next week. For this week, work on what you've got on your plate and the habits you need to tweak or completely renovate. Next week, you'll need to start meeting this prayer partner and helping each other along the way. Remember, this isn't a chance to one-up each other or condemn each other if you've gotten behind. This is a chance for you to fight alongside another fellow warrior in Christ who is seeking to become a dedicated disciple.

---

[23] Some guy named James, who was possibly Jesus' half-brother, said this one. Just check James 1:22.

Week 1 Assignment sheet

1. Daily Quiet time
    a. Daily prayer time
    b. Daily Bible reading/application
        i. Choose a highlight verse or phrase
        ii. Ask, "What does this mean?"
        iii. Ask, "What does it mean for my life?"
        iv. Ask, "What am I going to do about it?"

2. Scripture Memorization
    b. II Corinthians 5:17
        i. (Reference/verse/reference)

3. Prayer partnership—begin in one week

4. Quiet time log
    b. Turn this in to your disciple-maker at your next meeting. He/She will review and critique what you have done. This is not a place for them to get between you and God, but to measure your progress, and help ensure you're meeting with Him.

> "Therefore, if anyone is in Christ, he is a new creation. The old has passed away; behold, the new has come."
>
> II Corinthians 5:17 (ESV)

Lesson 2—

Building a Firm Foundation

In his book, *Making Sense Out of Spirituality*, Dr. Cliff Sanders recounts the time when he and his wife Becky were going to purchase a new home. At this stage in their lives, the couple knew they would not be able to afford a large home, but were surprised when their realtor presented them with the house of their dreams and told them it was in their price range. "It was a two-story home of over two thousand square feet, and it had great curb appeal[24]," he recounts.

As the couple took the initial stroll through the house, excitement grew. That is, until Cliff noticed water sitting in many of the floor vents, a sure sign of structural damage. Upon inspection from a professional, the prognosis was given with the worst possible results. The foundation of the house was in bad shape. What had appeared at first to be a house of dreams turned out to be a broken home that must now be avoided like the plague. As any honest realtor will tell you, structural issues are a deal breaker. No matter how pretty the building is that sits on a bad foundation, it is already headed for ruin. Sadly, this is the case with our spiritual houses, as well.

---

[24] Sanders, Cliff. *Making Sense Out of Spirituality*, MACU Press: Oklahoma City, OK, 2008, 7.

Best-selling author Ted Dekker once noted that "what you do will flow from what you believe[25]." The most basic foundational element of who we are and what we do comes from what we really believe about God. This is our foundation. This single element defines why we make the choices we choose to make every single day. What we believe about God is the lens we see the rest of life through, whether we realize it or not.

So what's the problem? If you're reading this book (especially after the scare of having to get disciplined), you likely already believe in Jesus Christ. Your foundation should be pretty solid, right? Perhaps. That's it. Just "perhaps." Maybe you really do have a strong foundation to build upon that has no cracks at all. But most people don't. Most people, even most Christians, have not taken the time to critically examine the foundation of their spiritual lives and radically test it against God's Word.

The average believer, even ones who have followed God for many years, has built the house of their spirituality on a foundation that has serious cracks throughout. This should be alarming to us. It should cause us to call for an inspection. That is exactly what this lesson is. You're going to be presented with the idea that your view of God is the very foundation upon which every other element of your faith is built.

I am a person who likes honesty, even if it hurts. Some call this a bit masochistic. The reality is, however, if you're going to get what God is giving you from this lesson, you have to be masochistic enough to completely tear down the spiritual house you've built over many years and critically re-evaluate your foundation. If it is found that your foundation is cracked, you have to be disciplined enough (with a caring group around you) to re-pour that foundation and

---

[25] Dekker, Ted. *The Slumber of Christianity: Awakening a Passion for Heaven on Earth,* Thomas Nelson: Nashville, TN, 2005, 199.

make sure it is done right before you allow *any* other piece of your spiritual house to stand again.[26]

So, if what we believe about God (really and truly, deep down) is the foundation of our spiritual life, why should we consider what we believe about God? Author William Temple strongly states, "If your conception of God is radically false, then the more devout you are the worse it will be for you...You had much better be an atheist[27]." Echoing that sentiment, Dr. Cliff Sanders (to whom this entire lesson is indebted) has stated, "If there is a God, it should be your life's business to know Him correctly for who He is and what He respects. The foundation for Christian living is knowing the kind of God that God really is."

If you haven't caught it yet, this is a really big hairy deal[28]. Having an incorrect view of God is like being on the wrong path towards a destination. The worst possible thing you can do if you're on the wrong path is to go further. Progress is actually found in doing an about-face and going back to where it all started. If you have an incorrect view of God, the worst thing you can do is become further devoted to this caricature or image.

All said and done, there are three reasons to consider what you believe about God. First, Christianity is reported to be a relationship. Christianity is not a series of rules that somehow makes you righteous before a Holy God...it is much more like a marriage covenant that impacts and sets the course of every moment of the rest of your life.

---

[26] Re-read that statement over and over until it sinks in. The longer you've been a Christian, the longer you need to spend re-reading it.

[27] Temple, William. *Christian Faith and Life*. MacMillian: New York, NY, 1931, reprinted 1936, 24.

[28] Try picturing a really big hairy deal. Draw what yours looks like in the margins. It's fun.

Secondly, trust and commitment are the result of knowledge. Psalm 9:10 says, "...and those who know Your name will put their trust in You." In Biblical times, the word "name" implied more than just what a person was called when listed on an attendance roster. A name implied something about who they were. It explained the character of the person. The Bible spends an awful lot of time showing, explaining, and revealing the character of God. Our trust in Him is a result of knowing what sort of Person God is. In all honesty, we will only trust God to the degree that we trust His character.

Third, this is the cry of the human heart. There is an aching in every human being that wants to be known and loved for who they really are. As I've found in the Scripture, God is no different. We are simply mirroring Him in this aspect. The reason God has given mankind the free will to accept or reject Him is because He didn't want a world of robots. God wanted a creation that could intimately get to know Him for who He really is.

As I claimed above, many people have a bad foundation. I would not hesitate to say that even a majority of those who call themselves Christians today have a serious flaw in the foundation of their spirituality. But, if this is true (which you'll discover in just a moment) then how did we get this problem? How did our view of God get distorted?

There are two primary answers to this question. The first place we got a distorted view of God was from significant relationships early in life. Social scientists have discovered that much of how we see the world is shaped very early on by our relationship with our parents, or lack thereof. To this end, your view of God is often a direct result of your early relationship with your father[29]. The

---

[29] Having recently become a father, this thought scares the poop out of me. Yes, poop is the most utterly spiritual word I could think of there.

more striking reality, however, is that the basic structure of your personality was almost entirely formed by your fifth birthday.

If your father was distant as a young child, you'll find in your life that God, no matter how devoted to Him you are, often seems very distant. If your father was cruel and punished you for every little transgression, you'll find that you see God as always out to get you for every wrong (no matter the size). As unfortunate or fortunate as you may have been in your early relationship with your father, that relationship has left ripples that daily affect the very way you see and interact with God.

The second area where we develop a distorted view of God is through uncritically reflecting on life. Critical thinking is not taught to growing minds any longer. As a result of this, so much of what happens to us in our lives is left uncritically considered and improperly worked through[30]. One example of this happens often to those who have lost a loved one in a tragic occurrence. Very likely, someone will come up to this person and tell them that it was just "God's will," or that "God needed another angel up in heaven for some reason we simply can't grasp this side of heaven."

We often give too much emphasis to "God's will" (and ironically not enough in other instances and areas). Biblically, there are three "wills" in the universe. God's will is, of course, one of them. Your own will is a second. Then there is the will of the enemy, who is called "the destroyer." The simple fact from Scripture is that God designed life to be a system where the will of man can thwart the will of God. Look at the Parable of the Sower and the Seed for an example of this.

When significant events happen in our life that we cannot explain, we simply chalk it up to God's will as a way of dealing with it (in a way that we really don't have to deal with it). Dr. Sanders says of this, "Many people begin to ascribe to God all of the terrible

---

[30] Usually on Facebook or Twitter.

things that have happened in their lives...He is the answer to the unthinkable, and the sense for the senseless events in life...If we cannot explain it, we assume that God did it[31]." In doing this, we often attribute events to the character of God that are not really His doing or even go against his character. We uncritically reflect on life and come out with a fault in our foundation because of it.

So how do we know if we have a distorted view of God? Only critical reflection and a revelation from the Holy Spirit will show the way. The following, then, must be critically reflected upon as you ask the Holy Spirit to guide you and, like an inspector, reveal the cracks in your foundation along the way. There are five very common misconceptions about what sort of God, God is. These five distorted views of God leave your foundation, and therefore everything built on that foundation, cracked and ready for demolition. What follows can serve as nothing more than a summary of these distortions. Due to this fact, I strongly recommend picking up and reading Dr. Cliff Sanders' *Making Sense Out of Spirituality*, and J. B. Phillips' *Your God is Too Small*[32].

The summary of the five distortions begins with God as the Cosmic Cop. This distortion sees God as a vindictive policeman waiting for you to do something wrong so He can "get" you. Others correlate this God to an image of Zeus in the sky hurling lightning bolts down upon those who don't do his every whim. This is a very common way that people mistakenly see God in their lives.

Think critically for a second. When you think of God, do you think of a God who is simply waiting for you to screw up so He can punish you? This god does not exist. This is not God as He is revealed in the Bible and it is dangerous to see Him in this light.

---

[31] Sanders, 24.

[32] My first reaction to Phillips' book was, "This book is too small." Seriously, it is like a hobbit compared to most books. I guess dynamite really can come in small packages.

Dr. Sanders says, "No intimacy or relationship is ever established with someone whom you fear and wish only to keep from punishing you.[33]" The Bible does tell us that we are to fear God and that this is the beginning of understanding, but I challenge you to do an etymological study on the word used that we translate as "fear" and what nuance it has against the kind of fear that makes God look like the boogeyman. Fear in the sense of the cosmic cop jails our relationship with the true God and works to separate us from Him through iron bars.

The second distorted view of God is that of "the voice inside my head." This is essentially breaking God down into the function of your conscience. God has given human beings a wonderful function in our neural pathways that helps us in so many ways to discern good and evil. Conscience, when broken down etymologically, literally means "with knowledge." This is that little pinprick of insight and knowledge you feel when you perceive that something you've just done (or considered doing) is not right. The problem is, our consciences can become malformed.

J. B. Phillips points out that many people have confused the function of their conscience with the action of God[34]. Our conscience, like everything in life, can be molded to one extreme or the other. When perfectly in harmony with how God designed it, our conscience can be a tool that warns of actual spiritual danger[35]; however, it can also become neglected until it is dull and unaware. Like Pharaoh in his dealings with Moses, our consciences can become scarred and seared by the sin we allow into our lives. Think of, in an extreme example, serial killers, who often admit they have felt nothing wrong in their actions. Sin can scar our conscience and

---

[33] Sanders, 31.

[34] Phillips, J.B. *Your God is Too Small,* MacMillian Publishing, New York, NY, 1961.

[35] Like a Spider-sense.

beat it like tough leather into a shape where it will not function properly.

Likewise, our conscience can become hypersensitive. Many people who view God as the Cosmic Cop also have hypersensitive consciences. To them, every little misstep is worthy of the most severe punishment. What a healthy conscience could overlook, a hypersensitive conscience will enslave a person's mind and emotions over, gripping it with fear and regret.

In both directions, when we confuse God with the function of the conscience He created in us, we allow ourselves to attribute things to God that are not Him. This leads to huge cracks in our foundation that will slowly destroy the very walls of the spiritual house we've built atop it. This is why we must, in a moment, look at what a healthy view of God should include.

A third misconception of the character of God is to see Him as the Pharaoh god. Pharaoh was an unrelenting taskmaster who pushed his servants and cared little for their well-being. A person who sees God in this manner never feels like he is enough, no matter what he does. No matter what task is accomplished, there is always a fresh one waiting at the end of a cracked whip. In this person's mind, his worth before God is based upon what he can do and it lasts only as long as he can continue to produce. Once he/she is unable to "do," God no longer has any need of them[36]. This is the God of 110%. Like an overzealous coach He demands we give Him more than we have and will never understand why we were unable to comply.

The fourth common misconception is what Dr. Sanders has called "the farmer and his mule." This misconception is very similar to the one we just discussed, with one slight but meaningful difference. "The farmer and his mule" god cares for us and tends to us (unlike the god of 110%), but he does so only that we may continue to serve him. This is a cuddlier pharaoh, but a pharaoh

---

[36] Insert scene from _____ movie with _____ villain here.

nonetheless. In this misconception, we are cared for and loved to a degree, but we must produce something to keep the love coming. This god may not require 110%, but his love is still contingent upon our production schedule.

The person who sees God in this way serves God not because He does value them, but to *become* valuable in God's eyes. This person is caught up in becoming a human doing instead of a human being. Service to God is real and God loves them to a degree, but the focus of the matter is staying valued in God's eyes. This is like the middle child who must walk in their older sibling's large shadow, yet does not get the glowing adoration of the youngest child. This child does as much as they can to become as valued (in their eyes) as their older sibling, rather than simply being themselves and being valued for who they are.

The final misconception we'll discuss is that of the Waiter God. You may call this the Server God if you prefer a gender-neutral term. In many ways, this is the opposite of the Pharaoh god. In this distortion, the balance has shifted to where God is the one who is always under a whip that we gleefully hold to torment Him. In this view, God exists to bring us what we want, when we want it. Not only is He the Creator of the universe, He is our divine waiter.[37]

This misconception has grown in popularity in many ways today. This is the god of "name it and claim it." This is the god of "God wants me to be happy, so…" In this twisted fantasy, God is so loving and so caring for us that He would never upset us in any way,

---

[37] Could you imagine God being your waiter? Sure, He wouldn't even have to ask you what you wanted (it would probably be on the table the moment you got there), but think of the tip you'd have to leave for literally perfect service. Who could even afford that? And, you can't stiff Him…he knows where you live.

shape, or form and will give us everything we ask the moment we ask it[38]. If we're honest, most of our prayers go to this false god.

Think about it, how much of your prayer time is spent before God as if He were Santa Claus and you've come before Him with a list of shiny toys you desire. It doesn't matter how "holy" this list may seem. This misconception runs deep in our "me" society. I know for myself, despite recognizing this misconception in my life, I often find my prayers to God sound something like, "And God do this… and God heal this…and God be with this…and God make this…" When you pray to a Waiter God for whatever your wish may be, you are praying to a figment of your willful imagination that does not exist. No wonder we often don't get what we pray for.

What comes next is the hardest thing you may ever have to do. Wherever your foundation includes any of the distortions of God that we've mentioned above, you cannot do anything less than remove the house of spirituality you've built atop it and ignite the dynamite. In all honesty, there are few who will not need to do this. Very likely this is going to be a lengthy process, and the more "religious" you've become in these misconceptions, the harder it is going to be for you. Take this seriously. If you don't take it very seriously, your spiritual house will crack and crumble. You may have built a pretty impressive spiritual house at this point in your life, but if that house has a bad foundation, it will not last.

Perhaps you need to stop, reflect, and critically think through what happens next. Maybe you need to spend a couple days journaling, talking with your pastor, seeking the guidance of your disciple-maker, or even getting counseling from a good Christian source. Whatever you do, the worst thing possible would be for you to ignore this. Make no mistakes; if your god looks like what is above, your god does not exist. Let me say that again. Say it out

---

[38] Of course, the devil sometimes gets in the way of this promised "immediate blessing" in this view. Pesky little devil.

loud and listen to every single syllable. If your god looks like what is described above, your god does…not…exist.

But, there is good news. In fact, the very message of the Bible (the Gospel) means "good news." The Bible spends a lot of time explaining the character of God. Don't get me wrong, there is a great deal of mystery surrounding the Lord that we may never understand this side of heaven[39], but the same God who desires us to enter into a true relationship with Him also took the first steps in explaining to us who He is. So much of the Bible is dedicated to this very subject, that it's utterly astonishing in scope.

In an effort to rebuild the foundation of our spirituality, we will briefly examine four aspects of God's character that are clearly described in Scripture. Please understand that what follows is simply a brief overview. If it should truly be our life's work to get to know God for Who He really is, then these serve as just the first whiff of what should become a much deeper study in your life. Each aspect discussed here deserves many books written about them (and, in fact, many books have been). Of course, the most important of these books is the source material itself, which we will now examine to find just Who is revealed in those powerful pages.

If we are to come to understand God for Who He really is, we must first understand that He is consistent with the Person of Jesus Christ. Hebrews 1:1-4 lets us know that Jesus the Christ is the exact representation of the nature of God. Even a cursory glance at the Gospels will show Jesus Himself making this exact claim. What this means for our understanding of God is that how we see Jesus interact in the Gospels is the exact way that God interacts with people. When we see Jesus speaking and dealing in a certain manner, we are seeing God act in that manner.

---

[39] Actually, there's this pretty awesome scene in Revelation with these thousand-eyed angels that still find new things to praise God for all the time…so maybe not even with an eternity in heaven.

Jesus said, "I and the Father are One," and, "He who has seen Me has seen the Father." This should make our hearts race. Unlike the pantheon of nameless gods invented and served from the dawn of time, we can see how the One true God interacts with people just like us. When we see how Jesus responds to the woman caught in adultery, we see exactly how God deals with us in our weakness. Likewise, when we read dialogue such as the scathing remarks Jesus gives in Matthew 23 to the religious of His day, we see exactly how God deals with us in our pride.

John 1:18 says that though we have not seen God, Jesus has *translated* Him to us. That's some powerful language. When we see Jesus act, we see the very movement and breath of our God. Therefore, a proper understanding (foundation repair) of the character of God is to first look at the life of Jesus the Christ. If our understanding of the character of God varies at all from the Bible's presentation of Jesus Christ, we have not seen the God who is and we must rebuild our foundation.

The second thing we come to in Scripture is a God who has our best interests at heart. Far from being the Cosmic Cop who is only out to get us when we do wrong, God truly cares about us enough to want only what is best for us. Many people do not believe, at the core of their being, that God has their best interests at heart. John 10:10 informs us (through the very mouth of Jesus Christ) that the Lord desires to give us life abundantly.[40]

In the original language of the Bible, there were at least two words we translate to mean "life" in English. One of these words, bios, carries a meaning of physical life. If Christ's words were that He came to give us bios abundantly, then we could only infer that He came to give us a life defined by duration. However, the word

---

[40] Don't mistake what I'm saying. Christ is clear that real life ONLY comes with our picking up our crosses and following Jesus daily. Life only comes through the death of our selfish desires.

used for life in John 10:10 is zoë, a word that has to do with the *quality* of life. Zoë is a more spiritual form of life. "God knows how life works, and, far from being eager to punish us, He wants us to enjoy life to the fullest.[41]"

The ancient Hebrews used to believe that God created life to work a certain way, and that wisdom was found in discovering how God intended life to be lived and so living it. God created life and understands what is best for us. Like a wise parent who can see what their child cannot, God does not do things to dampen our fun, but to keep us from what will truly destroy us. God has our best interests at heart.

This is not a warm and cuddly caricature of a god that does not exist. God created life for His good pleasure and blessed us to enjoy it. This does not mean that life was somehow created for us or that we can take this to mean whatever we want it to mean. God clearly outlined the rules in many areas, and we are to follow them or face the consequences of our missteps. But, God did not give us these guidelines to ruin our lives or to pile up heavy burdens on our backs, but to help us to have lives to the fullest. This aspect of God is tempered by the next dominant attribute of God.

The third understanding we must come to in rebuilding our view of God is that God is a God of Holy Love. The depth of those words is yet to come. In my home state of Wyoming, wind would often bend and warp sapling trees as they grew. Tension wires would have to be attached to them from four posts in order to make them grow properly. If the tension on these wires were not perfectly balanced, the tree would grow skewed in one direction and possibly have to be cut down.

Our understanding of the next aspect of our view of God must carry this same tension. The Bible very delicately balances the fact that God is holy, holy, holy, and that He is love incarnate.

---

[41] Sanders, 42.

Emphasizing one or the other of these two facts gives us a god who does not truly exist. Here is where, perhaps, the most damage has been done in our world when it comes to the character of God. Emphasizing God's holiness at the expense of His love gives us a caricature of God who is dominantly wrath and judgment. On the other hand, emphasizing God's love over His holiness gives us the God of popular culture who would never call us to do anything difficult or call anything we so dearly love "sin." This god would never be strict with us, never tell us we're wrong, and never create hell as a consequence for angels or humans who have openly rebelled against Him, because He is love. Or so the reasoning goes. Neither of these extremist gods exist. At all. Not even in the slightest.

We must, as the Bible does, come to an understanding of a God in perfect balance in His love and His holiness. Holiness means that He is without stain or blemish, perfect in every regard. We see this aspect of God shouted in glory in the book of Revelation. Revelation 4:8b says, "Holy, holy, holy is the Lord God almighty, Who was and Who is, and Who is to come[42]." Holiness means that God cannot accept anything that is stained or has sin. This is why we see in the Bible where the Hebrews had to make sacrifices for their sins regularly, because God cannot accept anything imperfect. This is the very reason we needed a Savior and the other side of this is the very reason why God provided the answer for us.

1 John 4:8 says, "Anyone who does not love does not know God, because God is love." God does not simply provide love. He *is* love. Love is an aspect of God's character. There is no true love apart from God, for love is a part of Who God is at His core. All "love" that we as humans share is borrowed capitol from the character of God. Again, this is why God provided a Savior for us. It is also why we're

---

[42] The ones saying this are actually those thousand-eyed angels I mentioned earlier. I'm telling you, you really need to check this one out.

even able to love Him in return. The Bible says that we love God because He first loved us (1 John 4:19).

Here is where I must digress for just a moment, however. Simply because "holiness" is somewhat foreign to our daily language and way of thinking, we actually seem to understand it better. We tend to have only one definition or so, even if we don't fully understand it. The term has not become watered down in disparity. Love, however, has. In the same breath we will say that we "love" our spouse, and also "love" a piece of clothing or a car. A man will say, "If you really loved me, you'd do it yourself and let me watch football," and a child will say, "But, don't you love me?" to a parent who will not buy them a new toy. Clearly, the word "love" carries quite a bit of baggage. Many people, especially those who do not want to be bothered to get to know God further than "God is love," read whatever meaning they want into the word.

This is why so many people are confused on the matter. In order to fully understand God as love, you need to be able to understand what true love is. Nicely enough, understanding the balance that holiness has in tempering love can help you to understand what love itself is. Love does not mean permission. Love does not mean veiled lust. Love does not mean whatever you happen to want it to mean. The Bible has a lot to say about love, so in your search for truth (another aspect of God, which we will not dive deeply into here) this could be a great jumping off point.

Of course, the "love chapter" in Corinthians would be a good place to start for personal study. In this regard, since 1 John 4:8 lets us know that God is love, we can also take the word "love" in 1 Corinthians 13 and replace it with the word "God" to see deeper aspects of God's character as love. God is patient. God is kind…etc. It works remarkably well and proves consistent with the remainder of Scripture.

In any case, the point here is that there must be a delicate tension between love and holiness if you are to have a correct view of God.

"Our view of God must have just the right tension between holiness and love. We dare not emphasize one to the neglect of the other. Both must be equally present if we are to have an accurate view of God.[43]" Anything less than this and you no longer have the God Who is.

The final aspect of God's character that we will use to rebuild our Spiritual foundation is the understanding of a God who is consistent with the revelation of Father. One of the most revolutionary things Jesus ever did was to tell humanity that they could relate to God as Daddy. In the history of the Hebrew people (who tended to overemphasize God's holiness, unlike those today who tend to overemphasize His love), you will find that God's name was regarded as so very holy that they would not write it or even speak it at times. In texts where God's name was meant to be, they would often leave it blank, take out all the vowels (which is where we get YHWH and the attempt to reconstruct it in Jehovah), or use the appellation Adoni. Even in speaking, the Hebrews would often not refer to God, but put an audible pause where His name was meant to be and then utter, "may His name be praised.[44]"

Contrast this with Romans 8:15 or Jesus' discourses in the book of John, which tell us to cry out to Him as Abba, Father. Jesus, in teaching on how we are to reference God, often used the term Abba. In today's world, we have over-glorified the simplicity of that word. Abba was what an Aramaic child would have uttered before (s)he could pronounce the term used in their language for "father." Literally, if Jesus' words were to be translated for meaning into English, He was saying that we can call God "Dada." In contrast to the great and overly reverent tone the people of God before Him

---

[43] Sanders, 44.

[44] Think along the lines of the way no one would say "Voldemort" in the Harry Potter movies. Though for very different reasons, I hope.

would take with the Creator, Jesus came and told us that we have a personal Father.

The imagery involved makes me think of a little child that is just learning to walk. I picture a child who is stumbling with his/her arms in the air raised to the one whom he trusts and finds complete comfort in as he sputters out, along with drool, the only thing his feeble mouth can utter, "dada." The imagery really is striking. If you understand the depth of that imagery, it is no wonder the religious wanted to kill Jesus. No wonder they thought He was blaspheming the name of God.

A firm and true foundation is one that understands to the very core that God is our Dada, a completely holy and completely loving Dada who has our best interests at heart. When combined with an understanding that Jesus Christ is the exact representation of God's character, we then have a foundation upon which we can build our spiritual house. This should be the start of your extreme makeover.

Take some time this week, maybe half an hour a day, and search through the verses mentioned above and their surrounding contexts. Spend some time reading through the Gospels. This must now become the foundation upon which the rest of your thoughts and "religion" must be based if we understand that how we see God impacts every aspect of our lives down to how we think. If how we view God dramatically affects the persons we become, then this foundation of our faith is the most important thing in life we can focus our immediate attention on, and it is the single most impactful thing we can do to change the course of the rest of our lives.

Week 2 Assignment Sheet

1. Daily quiet time
   a. Spending time with God is the backbone of Discipleship.

2. Scripture memorization
   a. Review 2 Corinthians 5:17.
   b. Learn 1 John 4:8 and Revelation 4:8b.
      i. Remember to learn them word perfect from the list in the back, and state the verse reference at the beginning and end of the verse.

3. Prayer partnership
   b. This week you should be pairing up with another disciple or two from your group. Set in place a plan to meet (call, etc.) each other daily, praying for each other and keeping each other accountable.

4. Quiet Time Log
   b. Submit your Quiet Time Log to your disciple-maker for comment.

"The one who does not love does not know God, for God is love."

1 John 4:8 (NASB)

"Holy, holy, holy is the Lord God Almighty, Who was and Who is and Who is to come."

Revelation 4:8b (NASB)

Lesson 3—

Meaningful Moments with the Master

The Japanese raise a tree called the bonsai tree. It's beautiful and perfectly formed, although its height is measured in inches. In California, there is a forest of giant trees called the Sequoia Forest. One of these giant trees has been named "General Sherman." Steve Seaton tells me that it extends into the heavens some 272 feet and measures 79 feet in circumference. This one tree, if cut down, could supply enough lumber to build thirty-five five-room homes with perhaps a few billion toothpicks left over.

However, did you know that at one time "General Sherman" and the bonsai tree were the same size? When they were seeds, each of these trees weighed less than $1/3000^{th}$ of an ounce. The story behind the difference in the size of these trees gives us a good lesson for living. When the bonsai tree sticks its head above the earth, the Japanese pull it from the soil and tie off its tap and feeder roots. The result is a miniature dwarf looking tree. The seed that produced the "General Sherman," however, fell into the mineral rich soil of California and was nourished by the rain and sun. Its roots were allowed to go deep, and the result was a giant tree.

The thought is this: neither the "General Sherman" nor the bonsai tree has a choice in its destiny. We do. We can grow up into spiritually mature followers of the Messiah, or we can remain dwarfs, becoming miniature as far as our spirits are concerned. It all depends on how deep you allow your roots to go. Paul encourages us in Colossians 2:7 to be firmly rooted, built up, and established in our faith in the Christ. It is up to you to see that you go on growing in the Lord.

Now that we've blown up and restored the foundation of our very lives, it's time to move on to more practical habits that we can begin to absorb into our lives to truly begin the transformation process of becoming a disciple. We discussed in the last lesson that Christianity is reported to be a relationship with God Himself. If this is true, why is it that our life with God often looks very little like even our failed human relationships?

SomeOne desires to spend time with you every day. If you make an appointment, He will keep it...even though He is very important. Not only does He want it, but you need it; to spend quiet time alone with the Master of the universe[45]. God designed human beings with an innate need for time with the Source of our very breath. We need Him. But, unlike a powerful CEO running a multinational corporation with no time to spare for son or slave alike, God will always make time for us to meet with Him. He sees it as that important. Too bad we often don't[46]!

Just in case you're asking the question, allow me to briefly let you know why you need a regular quiet time with God. There are at least four reasons. First of all, a quiet time makes us aware of His presence. In Psalm 46:10, God commands us to "cease striving and know that I Am God." You may know this as "be still and know that I am God," if you're using a more dynamic translation of the Bible. In either case, the imagery surrounding the context of this passage is that of both creation and destruction. In it you see God's creative hand and the destructive hand of man. Out of both, God

---

[45] Steve Seaton deserves credit for writing that sentiment. Poetic, no?

[46] Just think about the fact that you would probably club a baby seal for personal time with _____, and yet, who are they compared to the One who designed and maintains every atom in that person's body?

simply asks us to cease and know. Stop the chaos in your day for just a few minutes, no matter how much of your time management grid is burning on the urgent side, and know God. We know Him only through spending time with Him.

When I was a teen in youth group, my youth pastor (Joe Ganahl) recounted a question his son once asked him. The question was something like "How do I know God's voice?" Joe responded by asking Timmy, "If I were to call home from somewhere else, would you know it was me?" Timmy agreed that he would. Joe continued, "If Gary (his roommate in college) were to call the house, would you know that it was him?" Timmy said that he would not. "Why not?" Joe asked. Timmy responded, "I know your voice."

Timmy (now simply Tim) would recognize his father's voice over that of an acquaintance because he spent time with his father. The same holds true for us. Time spent with our Abba makes us aware of His presence. Jesus said it as, "My sheep hear My voice, and I know them, and they follow Me" (John 10:27). It is up to us to cease striving, put aside the chaos of our lives for a moment, and just know that He is God.

Secondly, a time of waiting before God gives us renewed strength. Isaiah 40:28-31 gives us a clear picture of this. In this passage the Lord says, "...the Creator of the ends of the earth does not become weary or tired...He gives strength to the weary...though youths grow weary and tired, and vigorous young men stumble badly, yet those who wait for the Lord will gain new strength." Think of yourself as having an internal battery. In today's world, almost everything around us is portable and battery driven to some degree (especially our all-important cell phones).

The imagery I picture here is that of a low battery meter attached to our souls. Though we try and try to get quick charges off of any number of things that are not the source of our power, only by waiting before God will we truly get that recharge our souls so desperately need. We were designed to run off of the breath of

God[47] and we will drain out without regular recharging from Him. The fascinating thing, though, is that God will never grow weary or tired. Truly, we are hooking our souls up to something so much more cosmically powerful than even the sun itself. God will never run out.

Third, quietness with God leads to confidence. Isaiah 30:15 says, "In repentance and rest you will be saved, in quietness and trust is your strength." Comedian Brad Stine points out that in the world around us we have become all too focused on our seemingly innate lack of self-esteem. He humorously points out that rather than teaching youth the hard truths of life that lead to self-esteem, we shelter them and try to protect them from ever growing up. His conclusion is that if we were to come before the throne of God and realize that "the Creator of matter tells you that you matter, then we can have confidence and then we can have self-esteem[48]." Quietness before God leads to deep confidence.

The final reason a regular quiet time before God is important is that Jesus habitually made solitude with the Father a priority. If we are becoming disciples, Jesus is the rabbi we're hitching our lives to. Jesus made solitude with God a priority and a habit. One read through the Gospels will reveal that Jesus was a fairly busy guy[49]. He is always going from place to place and the most consistent adjective used is "immediately." As in, there's not much time for anything else

---

[47] See Genesis chapter 1. God gathers a bunch of dust into the shape of a man and then breathes life into that first human...and He didn't even need a breath mint.

[48] Stine, Brad. *Put a Helmet On,* Perpetual Entertainment Group: Franklin, 2003.

[49] As in, (insert famous pop star here) level fame. People were hounding him for much more than autographs, too. They wanted him to heal, cast out demons, restore life, teach them, and...you know...overthrow Rome in His free time.

so do it now. There was a very real sense of busyness about the formal ministry of this Jesus who is called the Christ.

And yet, Jesus was never frantic and rarely drained[50]. He was exasperated many times with crowd and follower alike, but rarely do we see His batteries running low. Mark 1:35 shows us why. "In the early morning, while it was still dark, Jesus got up, left the house, and went away to a secluded place, and was praying there." The more the crowds pressed in on Jesus, the more He would guard His time with the Father. Now, let me ask you this, if Jesus, Who was and is God in the flesh, needed to spend quiet time away with the Father…how much more do you and I need it? The very times in life when we draw away from God the most (the tragic and the busy) are the very times when we need to protect our time with God with the most ferocity.

Now we see the why, so what about the how I've been promising you? What do we even do in our quiet times before the Throne? There are at least three elements that should be a part of our regular quiet time. This list is, of course, not all-encompassing as to what elements *can* be a part of your quiet time. I would argue, however, you cannot have intimate fellowship with God without these three core elements. Those wishing to go deeper should look into other works, such as *Celebration of Discipline*[51] by Richard Foster, for a more detailed list.

The first element of our quiet time with God is reading from God's Word. As disciples of Christ, we believe that the Bible is the very Word of God. It is His message of redemption and revelation of Himself to this World. Not only is it the most important book in the history of the world from literary to spiritual, it is living and active

---

[50] Though it did happen. Just look at how passed out he was on that one boat ride.

[51] There's that dirty word again.

and able to divide our spirits from our bodies. The Bible makes many great claims about itself. History makes even more.

The Bible is God's manual for how life works. It is His love letter to His people. It is an autobiography of the Father, the Son, and the Holy Spirit. It is a history of the people of God. Somehow it is also where we find our place in life, as well. It is poetry. It is prophecy. It is history. It is a group of letters written to ensure that the people of God really "got" it. The Bible is a polemic declaring the truth. It is a judgment concerning evil.

All of these characteristics describe the Bible, and yet it is so much more. There has never been another book in the history of the world like this. For all their boasting, no other holy book out there is ALIVE as this one is; not the Koran, not the Talmud, not the book of Mormon. No other book is able to make such bold claims and then back them up with supreme confidence. God Himself breathed this book into existence. It is living because He is living and is making Himself known to us through these 66 combined books and letters.

Still, as we discovered in the introduction, all people are told at some point that they should read the Bible, yet few are shown how. What follows is simply an introduction to what should be a part of your Bible reading. It is by no means exhaustive. I strongly recommend that you pick up *How to Read the Bible For All It's Worth* by Gordon Fee, *Bible Study That Works* by David Thompson, *Methodological Bible Study* by Robert Traina, or a similar work to help you in learning what it means to (really) study the Bible.

Here are the pointers that I will share with you in your introductory quest to read God's Word. First of all, you need to use a version of the Bible that you can understand. There are many great versions of the Bible to be found. One of the most amazing things you'll find in a study of the history of God's dealings with His people is that He always spoke to them in the language of their hearts. When people were speaking Sumerian, God spoke to them through Sumerian. When ancient Hebrew prevailed, God spoke to His people through ancient Hebrew. As the Greek language took over the world, God made His revelations to people in Greek.

Rather than relying only on some divine language that we must learn before coming before God, God always comes to us in the language that is most native to our hearts. This is why I personally do not hold to any claims that any one version of the Bible that has been translated into English is more holy by nature. I do not believe that the King James is the only Bible God has spoken through, though I do believe it to be a great translation. That said, however, there is a brief set of rules that I do follow in looking at a translation.

One of the reasons we have so many versions of the Bible in English today is because translators often use different methods in their translation. Some try to be as accurate as possible and translate word for word from the original Greek, Hebrew, and Aramaic. Others, while trying to maintain the original meaning of the Word, seek to find dynamic equivalents that will be more easily understood by modern readers. One of the highest examples of "word for word" translation is that of the New American Standard Bible (NASB). While this version is the most accurate you can get to the original language, it is also choppy here and there and can be harder to read.

A very popular example of a more dynamic translation is that of the New International Version (NIV). This may be the most popular Bible in use today, but it is not nearly as accurate. The NIV attempts to get the meaning while "massaging" the sentence to be more dynamically readable. On the farther scale, we find transliterations and paraphrases. Here you will find versions like "The Message." I do not recommend using paraphrases as your primary Bible in study. I would say that these can be great to aid you in understanding, but should be used as aids only.

For myself, I prefer to stick to the more literal translations. Some of these include NASB, English Standard Version (ESV),

King James Version (KJV), New King James Version (NKJV), and the New Revised Standard Version (NRSV). What it comes down to, however, is that you need to find a Bible that speaks in the language of your heart while still paying attention to accuracy. You need not read from a specific version simply because someone once told you only one version is "holy" (as is common in KJV only churches[52]). Just be sure what you're reading carries that balance between accuracy and readability.

The second pointer in reading from God's Word is to mark and write in your Bible as you read. This may sound like blasphemy to you. Certainly, many people are taught to never even crease a page on their Bible because it is so holy. While it is true that it is the most holy of all books, this comes down to intimacy with Christ. Just as Christ took _____ (may His name be praised)[53] and told us that we could relate to Him as "Dada," the Bible can become an intimate tool for communion with God, while still being revered as holy. Marking and writing increases the likelihood that you'll remember what you've studied, and can then become a place of remembrance signifying what has been crucial to you in the past.

Along these lines, I recommend using an inexpensive Bible for your quiet time reading, one that you will not mind marking in, highlighting certain passages, and etc. There is nothing wrong with having a "nice" Bible that you keep in pristine shape and revere, but you'll find great rewards from looking back through a Bible that has been marked up with notes and insights. So, when you're in your quiet time before God, read until you find a verse or passage that speaks to you, and mark it!

---

[52] Some of these churches, while meaning well on the holy/love scale, make me feel like God stopped speaking to people in their language when Shakespeare died.

[53] Just to clarify, "Voldemort" does not go in this blank. Just making sure you're still with me on that one.

Now that you know how to keep your Bible study exciting, so to speak, you'll likely need some pointers on where in your Bible to read. If reading the Bible is fairly new to you, start by reading the New Testament. At some point, you will certainly need to delve into the rich waters that the Old Testament provides, but initially start in the pages of the New.

When you're reading, finish reading all of one book before you start another. This is certainly a hard practice for many Christians who have a form of spiritual ADD[54]. The tendency today is to "skip around." While, you'll find that God shows up even if you skip around in the Bible, reading all of one book ensures that you're more likely to catch the broader context that various topics and verses reside in.

Perhaps the greatest mistake people often make in reading Scripture, especially in doing "memory verses" and such, is taking a verse and stripping it of its context. But, like Dr. Bauer at Asbury Theological Seminary says, "Context is everything." Taking the Bible out of context can lead to everything from terrible theology to open rebellion against the intent and purpose of a verse. While this risk is there even when reading a whole book, reading in context will help to frame the statements Scripture makes and dramatically reduce the chance of taking things terribly out of context.

Learning to read in context is key to understanding Scripture. My favorite example of this is Philippians 4:13. Philippians 4:13 says, "I can do all things through Him who strengthens me." It is one of the verses, if not the primary verse, taken out of context the most in today's world. So many people read this and imply into the text that they can fly, they can start a new business, they can

---

[54] If you took the time to look at this footnote as soon as you came across it, you probably don't struggle with Spiritual ADD. If you're only seeing this because you happened to see it at the bottom of the page...squirrel.

_____[55] through Christ. If you take the words themselves and divorce them from their context, this may be a valid reading; however, the immediate context of the verse shows that Paul was speaking of the ability to be content in any situation that God and life send our way. Whether in poverty or in riches, in hunger or in fullness, I can do all things through Christ who strengthens me.

Another suggestion is to avoid reading the Gospels in consecutive order. There is certainly nothing wrong with reading through Matthew, Mark, Luke, and John back to back if you're doing a character study on Christ, seeking to piece together the synoptic gospels[56], etc. For the average reader, however, going through the gospels back-to-back can lead to overlap and perhaps even a drop in focus. Even though each Gospel has its own wonderful nuances, the new believer may find them repetitive if done in sequence.

Likewise, I do not recommend starting in Genesis and reading through Scripture consecutively if you're new to Bible study. Genesis and Exodus are remarkable books, but the average young believer will begin to lose interest or get completely lost and confused by the time Leviticus and Numbers roll around. Going through the Bible in order is a great thing to do later in your walk, but early on you will want to read different books.

Which brings me to the next point: in the early phases of your Bible study avoid books that are difficult to understand. I would not want a new disciple to begin their study in Revelation or Leviticus, for example. Each is a wonderful book with powerful things that God is wishing to convey, but tackled early on they can simply confuse and derail a well-meaning Bible study. The idea of studying Revelation may entice some, due to the Apocalyptic nature of the

---

[55] More fun with fill-in-the-blanks. I should write one of those Mad Libs books.

[56] The word "synoptic" means "with one eye", and refers to Matthew, Mark, and Luke. Poor John, he doesn't get to be part of the group.

work, but until you've struggled through those sections of the Bible that lead to better immediate understanding, I wouldn't suggest distracting yourself with those parts that take such amazing depth of theological context and insight to fully understand.[57]

A good place to begin for a new disciple would be the writings of John, Mark, James, Psalms, and Proverbs. These are often more direct and easier to comprehend as you build a context of the greater Bible in your mind. However, even the "easier to understand" books of the Bible will often have some more difficult spots. Initially, though certainly not later on in your walk, you may wish to skim over these more difficult sections, such as the "begats," which are long sections of lineage.

If you're stumped on where to start, one way to read through the Bible is to read a Psalm and a Proverb a day for a half a year to a year. Since there are perfectly thirty-one chapters of Proverbs, you'll pretty much read through the entire book once each month and there is a wealth of wisdom to be found in Solomon's teachings. Likewise, the Psalms are some of the most gutturally and emotionally honest Scriptures you'll find[58]. These often prove to be a source of great refreshment for those whose souls have come under doubt or persecution.

The first step in a quiet time with God is to read from His word. Not only did Jesus make a practice of this in His life, but all great followers of Him since have as well. Time spent with God in His Word proves to have a plethora of good effects in our lives, and

---

[57] If you really feel the need for that "end of the world" mania, pick up Jason Boyett's amazing *Pocket Guide to the Apocalypse.* You'll laugh, you'll cry, and you won't even notice that you're learning a ton along the way.

[58] The way in which David seems to call out God at times is just one of those places where if Christianity were a "safe" religion, these moments would not be included or would be modified greatly. David basically says, "God, you suck" at one or more points, but always comes back to how great God is. God is honest. His book is honest enough to share such vulnerable moments.

as Steve Seaton says, "A Bible that is falling apart often belongs to someone who isn't."

The second thing we must learn to do in our quiet time is to apply God's Word. This, I would say, is the single most overlooked area in the Christian faith. As we've seen, too many people know innumerable truths and yet have applied very few of them to their daily life. Discipleship is application of God's Word to our lives. This is an essential part of the process. James 1:22 tells us that we are not to be merely hearers of the Word, but doers. Likewise, Matthew 5:19 tells us that it is he who practices God's commands who will be considered great in the Kingdom of Heaven.

Don't be confused, there is nothing you can do to earn your way to heaven. There is not a single thing you could do to make yourself righteous before God. The Bible teaches that our attempts at righteousness before God are like dirty used menstrual cloths before Him[59]. There is none who is righteous, no not one. We are saved by grace alone through faith alone. Still, James tells us that faith without works is dead.

There is no contradiction here. James does not teach that works save us. He simply lets us know that if we truly have a living faith in God, it will compel us to obey Him and do good works. We can see from our works if our faith is really alive or not. The trick is in going from merely reading God's Word and telling ourselves that we've done a good thing to actually doing what it says. When I was a student at Asbury Theological Seminary, the motto was, "Where head and heart go hand in hand." This is the imagery we're talking about. If God's Word has not traveled from your head to your heart, you have not embraced the greater power of God's truth, and if this has not traveled from your heart to your hands, your faith is dead.

---

[59] Check out Isaiah 64:6. That's actually what it says...well, ok... it says "filthy rags" in most translations. But, that's what the filthy rags were. Remember that honesty thing I was talking about.

In learning to apply God's Word to our daily lives, we must learn to take the timeless principles that the Bible is teaching and seek to understand what they mean for us today. Again, I recommend *Bible Study That Works* as a tool to teach you how to find what timeless principles exist in the passages you read. A simple way to do this is to read until you find a verse or phrase that is clearly sticking out to you. Once God lays such a verse before you, start by asking yourself, "What truth is God's Word teaching in this?"

As a part of your Quiet Time Logs you are asked to enter this process. On your sheet, write down the verse (or verse reference if it is lengthy) that God is drawing your heart toward. Then, ask yourself, "What truth is God's Word teaching in this?" Answering that question means you need to have looked at the context of what is going on. You may even need to look up a good Biblical dictionary or Biblical encyclopedia. Several of these are available for free online. Next, ask, "What is God trying to say to *me* through this? What does it mean for *my* life?" This question takes the timeless truth that God's Word is teaching and directly connects it to the situation in life that you yourself face.

Once you have assessed what God's truth is speaking directly to you in your situation, ask, "What am I going to do about it?" This is the trick, right here. This last question, if followed through, is what separates the men from the boys, and dead faith from living. Once you've seen the truth of the matter and know what God is asking from you, you have to do something about it. A good thing to do would be to give yourself a measurable goal and write that down.

You don't want to fall into the trap of making applications like, "I'm going to be more loving." What does that even mean in a practical sense? How are you going to do that? A more fitting application would be to say, "Today, before I go to bed, I am going to perform one loving act for _____[60]." Be specific. Be measurable. Then do it. The problem, on the whole, with today's Christianity is not that we are under-informed about what the Gospel requires of us, but that we have not taken the Bible seriously when it says it requires action. The Bible says things like, "Crucify your sinful desires," and we think it's just being cute. What would happen if we really lived like it was asking something tangible from us?

To review, your quiet time before God should include both the reading of His Word, and application of it to your life. The third thing you should have as a part of your regular quiet time is prayer. We will devote a much larger section to prayer in a coming lesson. For now, pray for strength and guidance from Him. Pray that He will reveal His will to you and give you the strength to do it.

There are many methods of praying. You may wish to pray the prayer Jesus gave us during His Sermon on the Mount[61]. You may wish to use the ACTS method of prayer, by which you begin in adoration (reminding yourself how great God is), confession (telling God exactly how you have fallen short), thanksgiving (being thankful for what you have), and ending with supplication (asking for your needs). You may also pray Scripture itself back to God. The Psalms are great tools for this, but they are not the only Scriptures you could use. In this, you simply prayerfully read back the written Word to the Author.

You may also simply wish to sit in silence and listen to God. Certainly, many thousands of monks and prophets have found this to be a most meaningful form of prayer across the centuries. As a part of this, you may simply tell God that you love Him and

---

[60] Dare I point your attention to yet another fill-in-the-blank opportunity? I think I shall. Or is it, "I think I can, I think I can?"

[61] The one that starts out, "Our Father, Who art in heaven…" and ends with the Green Goblin taunting Aunt May. Sorry, I guess that's already an outdated movie reference. How did I get so old already?

await His response. However you pray, prayer must be a part of your time with God. Jesus modeled this, as has every saint that followed Him since.

Before we conclude this lesson, I must briefly give you a few quick and practical pieces of advice in making this quiet time happen. First of all, decide what time of the day you are able to be the most attentive or alert and set that as your quiet time. Some people feel that the most spiritual thing they can do is start their day off with God. Others find solace in giving the quiet of the evening over to Him. The reality is that whatever time you are the most alert and able to set aside without distraction should be your designated time. You'll find that the best part of your day, or "first fruits," is often the only one you can control.

Be sure to find the place that is the most conducive to alertness and quietness, free from distractions. You should not have your quiet time in front of the TV while watching the morning news. You need to have a place that is free from clutter and distractions; otherwise, you risk giving God a minimal amount of your attention. Some people have a quiet room they can set aside, others a quiet meadow, or a backyard. Wherever you can free yourself from distractions is where you should make your quiet time location.

Lastly, you need to be sure to have a set duration when you first start out. Some people, in their initial joy of discipleship, lose many hours in their quiet time with God. More likely, you find it a struggle and only set aside a minute here and there. In my opinion, you should give God no less than 15 minutes in quiet time a day. There are 96 fifteen-minute periods in every day. If you give God less than that, you're giving Him less than $1/96^{th}$ of your day[62]. Is it any wonder you and I don't look much like Christ with that sort

---

[62] I promised I wouldn't make *you* do any more math…but think of how fun it would be to have someone else figure out how many fifteen minute periods (and therefore portion out of 96ths of a day) one spends if they were

of commitment? Length does not always determine the value of a quiet time. Some people will find in half an hour before God what others would not find in weeks, but there needs to be some sort of an expectation going in that you will spend no less than 1/96th of your day in quiet time with God (15 minutes).

What will your goal be? Some people prefer a half an hour. Others are able to give a whole hour. Some will struggle to get fifteen minutes. Whatever your goal will be is up to you, your ability, and your personal schedule. It takes fifteen minutes to start; _____ will be your goal. Whatever your goal may be, just do it.

---

to watch just one extended *Lord of the Rings* or *Hobbit* movie. The results are likely staggering.

Lesson 3 Assignment sheet

1. Daily quiet time
    a. Put into practice the principles discovered in this lesson.

2. Scripture meditation
    a. Review 2 Cor 5:17, 1 John 4:8, Revelation 4:8b.
    b. Learn John 15:7-8
        i. This is a bit longer block of Scripture than we've done so far. You will need to devote a little more time to learning it WORD PERFECT from the included sheet.

3. Prayer partnership
    b. Continue to meet with your prayer partner.
    c. Be sure to check up on each other and encourage each other to make bold commitments.

4. Quiet Time Log
    b. Turn in this week's quiet time log to your disciple-maker and begin a new one.
    c. If you are not getting all 7 days of quiet time in, discuss with your disciple-maker why. Have you set aside a regular time? What distractions are you facing? Apply the lesson above to your quiet time.

"If you abide in Me, and My words abide in you, ask whatever you wish, and it will be done for you. My Father is glorified by this, that you bear much fruit, and so prove to be My disciples."

John 15:7-8 (NASB)

Lesson 4—
Hiding God's Word

Have you ever wished days were just a little longer so you could get more done? I mean, surely, all that extra time would relieve the pressures of our chaotic world, right? With just a few more hours, e-mails would answer themselves, the yard would mow itself, and dogs and cats would immediately get along. Perhaps this is how you feel after reading through the last lesson. There just seems like so much to do.

Allow me a moment to encourage you. By this point in your discipleship journey you've looked at what it means to be disciplined to godliness, reformed the entire foundation of your life, and have memorized about five key Scriptures along the way. You've also learned some tips and tricks about coming before God in His Word and prayer. That's quite a bit to have done in just around one month. But, don't slouch back in your chair yet.

For this lesson, I want you to imagine with me a world like the ones portrayed in the film *The Book of Eli* or in the book *Fahrenheit 451*. Both of these works portray a futuristic world in which, for one reason or another, the Bible has been utterly wiped from the face of the planet. In *The Book of Eli*, for example, we see a world torn apart by war and decimated to ruins. In this world, only one lone warrior walks the face of the earth carrying with him the only Bible left in existence.

Without spoiling too much of the movie, Eli reads through the Bible every day for over 30 years. When the Bible falls into the hands of violent men who honor Scripture only because they know it can wrongly control and enslave a populace who is no longer familiar with the love it contains, Eli proves his mettle at the end of his long journey by reciting the King James version of the Bible, word for word, to the man controlling the last remaining printing press. In a world at war, Eli carried the Word of God in him, and saved it from oblivion.

In the Bible we find that we are in a world at war. The often neglected other half of John 10:10 (that we ourselves neglected earlier, ironically[63]) is that though God has come to give us zoë life, there is one who tries to steal, kill, and destroy you in any way emotionally, relationally, physically, or spiritually that he can. This is the devil, the enemy of our souls. Many people often picture him as the "little red devil" with a pitchfork and horns. The Bible paints an image, however, as one who comes to us as an angel of light and hides next to the truth (2 Corinthians 11:14). The greatest trick the devil has in his arsenal is to take truth and give you something just next to it. It's almost truth, so it looks enticing, but in it is the way to death and destruction.

The devil likes to make himself look just like one of your buddies[64]. And, as your "buddy," he'll whisper to you, "When you're faced with a busy day, save precious time by skipping your devotions." On paper we can see the lie in it right away, but when it's whispered in our ear in the heat of a busy moment, we almost believe that this is a message from a concerned friend. Between that and his use of our old ways to trip us up, satan is by far the worst "friend" we could ever have...and yet, too many times we let his voice into

---

[63] But are now rectifying...

[64] I think this is where people get that horrid "we'll share a cold one in hell" theology.

our lives. His entire M.O. is to seek to destroy us, the world around us, and the very Spirit of God within us.

In his work *Living Above the Level of Mediocrity*, Dr. Charles Swindoll has said:

> In order for old defeating thoughts to be invaded, conquered, and replaced by new, victorious ones, a process of reconstruction must transpire. The best place to begin this process of mental cleansing is with the all-important discipline of memorizing Scripture. I realize it doesn't sound very sophisticated or intellectual, but God's book is full of powerful ammunition! And dislodging negative and demoralizing thoughts requires aggressive action. I sometimes refer to it as a mental assault[65].

The simple fact is that by becoming disciples of the God of the universe we have set ourselves at odds with the prince of the air. Far from being complacent about this, he will attack your soul in any way he can to get you to stumble, fall, or turn away from this new life. The Word of God tells us that the Bible itself is the best weapon we have in combating this enemy. In more than one place, it is referred to as our sword.

This is the underlying reason for why memorizing Scripture is important. Scripture memorization gives us power to defeat the enemy. Psalm 119:11 says, "I have stored up Your Word in my heart that I might not sin against You." Obviously, the power of God's Word is meant to be stored in our hearts like a precious treasure. Just like Eli, we should seek to internalize God's Word as if it were the last remaining copy on the planet. Of course, each disciple will

---

[65] Swindoll, Charles R. *Living Above the Level of Mediocrity*, Word Books: Nashville, TN, 1987, 26.

only be able to do this in varying degrees[66], but we should all have this as our goal.

In addition to this, when Jesus Himself was tested in the wilderness by the devil, He always responded the same way: "It is written." Jesus, in human terms, was a product of a Jewish society where young men were required to have memorized (word for word) the majority of what we now call the Old Testament by the time they were thirteen…And you thought this book was rough for asking you to memorize a verse or two a week!

When Jesus was confronted by the devil himself in Luke chapter 4, He responded to every attack by quoting the Word of God that was stored in His heart. This is how we must equip ourselves as well! We are in a world at war with an enemy that desires to destroy our souls. Jesus internalized God's Word as a defense against the snares of the devil, and the great news is that we can too. Certainly, Jesus may have had a leg up on us due to the culture He was raised in (and the fact that He was God in the flesh[67]), but this does not excuse us from accessing the same power that Jesus used when tempted.

This is not the only reason we need to consider the importance of knowing God's Word. Hiding God's Word in our hearts also gives spiritual enrichment and the power to preserve our peace of mind. Colossians 3:16 says, "Let the Word of Christ richly dwell within you…" When we do this, according to Philippians 4:7, "the peace of God, which surpasses all comprehension, will guard your hearts and your minds in Christ Jesus." We must store God's Word in our heart. It is just as imperative as in the fictional worlds of *The Book of*

---

[66] When I was in college, I had a professor who had memorized something like 90% of the Bible. He would open his Bible, set it down in front of him before class, but wouldn't ever have to look at it to quote even the longest and most strange-name-laden portions of Scripture.

[67] Who invented…you know, words themselves…mouths…all of that.

Eli or *Fahrenheit 451.* This is why you've been memorizing Scripture as a part of this course.

Now, let's talk about how best to do this. There are ten tricks I'll share with you that will help you to store God's Word in your heart. Be sure to use these tricks and come back to this section in your memorization of the required verses. Especially with the longer verses, these will be helpful.

1.   Before you begin, read the verse out loud several times.

The more senses you involve in memorization, the better it will cling in your grey matter. If there were a way for you to smell a Bible verse, that would be helpful, as well, but since there is not a scratch and sniff Bible (and you would not want one if you were reading Ezekiel 4:12-15), seeing, speaking, and hearing the Word will be your primary mode of using your senses.

2.   Learn the reference and the phrase as a unit.

Rather than separating the verse reference from the words of the verse in your mind, learn them together. "Psalm 119:11 I have stored Your Word..." This will help make the verse stick in your mind and will make the verse reference easier to remember. Your brain is fully capable of separating them back out when needed.

3.   Learn each verse word perfect.

We've already discussed the reasoning behind this a bit. To further it, though, we have to get out of the habit of misquoting the Bible. As I mentioned, I am just as guilty of this at times. I could tell you up and down what many Scriptures mean, but have no luck in telling you where they are or what they say word for word. In the culture Jesus grew up in, scribes would copy the Bible by hand.

They knew how many letters every line on the page would have. If any line did not match up exactly, the entire page would be thrown away. They cared greatly for the exact accuracy of God's Word. We should too.

If ever a day came where the Bible was banned from the world and every last copy was burned, we should, as a discipled community, still be able to pass down the Scripture to the next generation. While I am not saying that every one of us can have the entire Bible memorized word for word (though that is certainly a lofty goal), I am saying we should strive to on some level. We should be concerned with the accuracy of the Word.

4. Begin adding phrase by phrase.

How do you eat an elephant? One bite at a time. If you come across a larger section of Scripture that you're going to memorize, learn it a phrase at a time for easier management. You may need to do this with one or two of the larger verses we have assigned during this course.

5. Work on the verses audibly as much as possible.

Again, this is involving as many of your senses as possible. When you work on your verses out loud, you speak and hear yourself speaking as well as reading them. This makes it much more likely that you will remember them.

6. As you memorize and review the verse, think about how it applies to your life.

There is a technique in memorization called "Creating a memory castle." Though I will not explain the ins and outs of this here, you are trying to associate what you're trying to memorize with a mental image or emotion, to have it stick with you. In this manner, think about how the verse applies to your life. This will create an emotional pull on you that will stick with you when you seek to recall the verse from memory.

7. Write verses on cards for convenient review.

Or, hang your verse sheet across from the toilet. Sounds banal, but works pretty well.

8. Once you have it, write the verse out by memory.

The best way to test yourself to see if you have truly hidden a verse in your heart is to take out a blank piece of paper, without first looking at your Bible, and write the verse out from memory. If you can do this word perfectly nine times out of ten, you've got it stored in your heart.

9. The most important element of Scripture memory is review, review, review.

The most important element of Scripture memory is review, review, review. That is, review. The more you go over something, the deeper it lodges itself in your heart. Additionally, associations can tend to weaken over time, reviewing what you're learning is the only way to keep it hidden deep in your heart for good.

10. Visualize.

This goes back to what was said above. If you can, picture what is going on in the verse. If it is from a story, picture the story. Give people faces and hair color. Picture Jesus (or whomever is speaking) mouthing the words as you go over them in your head. If it is not already there, picture something more abstract. For "Psalm 119:11 - I have stored up Your Word in my heart that I might not sin against You," you may wish to picture the cavern of your heart being opened by a shimmering key and God's Words being placed in there and locked back up with armed guards fighting against dark sin that is trying to creep its way in. Often times, the more concrete in some ways and abstract in others you can make this, the more memorable it will be.

In finishing up this lesson, I would like to leave you with some insights gleaned from a wonderful article by Charles Hummel entitled *The Tyranny of the Urgent*[68]. This will serve to sum up some things we've talked about in the past lessons, as well as solidify the needs in the current. If you can, read through the original article for deeper insight and clarity.

Often times, when we evaluate our busyness we find that our shortage of time can simply be misplaced priorities. The greatest danger in this is letting the urgent things in life crowd out the important. We already know that both Bible study and memorization are important tasks; we must now make sure that the urgent things that come up every day do not crowd them out. When we look at the life of Jesus we can see that although Jesus was able to say that He finished the work that God gave Him, His life was never frantic.

Jesus made time for the important things, even at the expense of the urgent things, at times. Look at the life (or death, rather) of Lazarus. Though it was urgent that Jesus come and heal him or risk Lazarus's death, Jesus kept to what was important and let the urgent need pass. Lazarus dies, but Jesus shows God's power by bringing him back to life. It is through prayerful meditation on God's Word that we gain His perspective on what is truly important.

---

[68] Hummel, Charles E. *Tyranny of the Urgent:* IVP Books, Downers Grove, IL, 1994.

We must also look at our motivations. In our lives, often times, we make frenetic service for God into an escape from God. The danger you'll see in entering into any discipleship course is that doing things for God can replace actual time with Him. Jesus never made this happen. He was able to enter quiet solitude with God regularly. We must pray for God's guidance. When we fail to pray, as Charles Hummel says, we are saying with our actions, if not with our lips, that we don't need Him.

This is the sum of the struggle you're likely facing so far in this course. Keep at it, because it will come to you. Remember, "It is God Who works in you to will and act according to His purpose![69]"

---

[69] Philippians 2:13. It also provides proper context for Philippians 4:13 to prevent misuse.

Lesson 4 Assignment Sheet

1. Daily Quiet Time
   a. Continue deepening your walk by cultivating your quiet time with God. Record your applications in your Quiet Time Log.

2. Scripture Memorization
   a. Review 2 Corinthians 5:27, John 4:8, Revelation 4:8b, and John 15:7-8.
   b. Learn Psalm 119:11, Psalm 119:105 (Word perfect).

3. Prayer partnership
   a. Continue to pray with your partner and provide encouraging accountability.

4. Quiet Time Log
   a. Submit this week's log to your disciple-maker and begin a new one.
   b. You should be getting all 7 days in at this point.

"I have stored up Your word in my heart, that I might not sin against You."

Psalm 119:11 (ESV)

"Your word is a lamp to my feet and a light to my path."

Psalm 119:105 (ESV/NASB)

Lesson 5—
My Relationship with Christ

Throughout my time in college and seminary, I was taught with some measure of precision to exegete the Bible. The word exegete means, simply, to draw meaning out of the Bible. The opposite of that, isegete, means to read meaning back into the Bible. Through various tools and the use of the Inductive Bible Study method[70], I came to a place in my life where I could break apart whatever passage of Scripture was before me in several different ways and put it back together again with a better understanding of the historical context, the original authorial intent, the importance of the original language of the text, and more.

The problem was, I came to replace actual time *with* Christ with simply studying *about* Him. I had done the needed work of rebuilding my foundation with God and then attempted to skip straight into building the attic, rather than starting with the living room, the kitchen, and other needed aspects. My time with Christ became something of an intellectual pursuit, rather than a conversation between two hearts. To be honest, while too few Christians come to discover the joys that such detailed study of God's Word can inject into their lives, when study for the sake of study becomes the basis

---

[70] It's ironic that IBS are the initials for both Inductive Bible Study and Irritable Bowel Syndrome, because after dozens of hours looking at one single verse those two terms start to come together in strange ways.

of our relationship with a Holy God, there's something important missing.

In his article, *The Jogging Monk and Exegesis of the Heart*[71], James Bryan Smith recalls a similar time in his own life. Being himself in the midst of a seminary education heavy in exegetical tools for studying the Bible, Smith became somehow worn down and distant from God. In an effort to reclaim the vibrancy of his relationship with Christ, Smith entered into a monastery and was assigned to "the jogging monk." Though Smith had expected "an elderly man, bearded to the knees," the man that entered was far from that description.

Upon meeting with "the jogging monk," his director gave him the simple assignment of reading the angel's interaction with Mary in Luke chapter 1. That was it. That was his assignment for the whole day. As Smith recounts, "I spliced and diced the verses as any good exegete would do, ending up with a few hypotheses and several hours to sit in silence[72]." Despite his "splicing," the jogging monk was not impressed. Rather than give him kudos for a great job dissecting the Word of God, the monk instead reassigned the same passage as his assignment for the entire next day. The same set of verses from one chapter of the Bible, for an entire day.

Only this time, he asked him to think about what God was saying to him. After much frustration, the monk again made the exact same assignment for a third full day. This time, however, Smith finally began to open up before God and see how what Mary had encountered in her time with the angel might just have some impact on his own personal life. What happened was that this seminary student went from "simple" exegesis of the text to allowing the text to also exegete his own heart.

---

[71] Smith, James Brian, *The Jogging Monk and Exegesis of the Heart*, Christianity Today, July 22, 1991, pp. 29-31.

[72] Ibid.

This brings us to our relationship with Christ. Responsible exegesis of the Word of God is paramount to a society that, at best, simply glances at the depths of Scripture. If we do not allow Scripture to examine us as we read it, we've missed the deep waters that God has for us. If do not allow the Scriptures to exegete our hearts as we read them, we miss the deeper relationship that Christ desires to enter into with us.

In John 15:15, Jesus tells us that He "no longer call(s us) servants...instead I have called you friends." It's very important that we understand the nature of our walk with Christ as His disciples. Having been "born again" (John 3:3) by accepting Christ, you have begun the most important pursuit of your life. John 15:15 reminds us that our walk with Christ is a relationship, not a religion. Just as "the jogging monk" pushed the seminary student into a deeper level of relationship with God, this lesson is designed to shed some light on your own relationship with Christ. This discussion is very important to enter into because, as we mentioned in lesson two, Christianity is reported to be a relationship.

Take a look through the Gospels and ask yourself who you would guess is most often cast in the villain role. More than likely you didn't even have to think before you came up with the Pharisees. But there's a problem with that. The Pharisees were never meant to be the bad guys. The Pharisees belonged to an elitist group in Jewish society whose purpose was to look for and prepare the way for the coming of the Messiah. They were supposed to be Jesus' welcoming committee. So why do we see them coming against Him and ultimately being the catalyst for satan's plan to kill Jesus? The fact of the matter is that the Pharisees (as well as the Sadducees, and Essenes in various degrees) became consumed with religion for the sake of religion rather than a relationship with God.

The fact that Jesus prioritized relationships over their religious rules (many of which they added to the Biblical texts or redefined to the point of exhaustion) drove them away from Him. In reality, these men who were supposedly awaiting the redemption of the Messiah worked to kill the very Man they were waiting for because they began to cling to religion rather than God. Perhaps you know of other followers of God who do the same. Maybe I'm describing a path you're already walking.

Whatever your case may be, the truth is that our walk with God is a relationship with His Son, not a set of rules that bind us up. Don't jump to too many conclusions, though. Jesus made it abundantly clear that if we are to be called His disciples then we must lovingly follow the commands and the will of His Father. The difference is that He called us to do this out of love, not out of blind devotion to rules for the sake of rules.

We have to enter a love relationship with Jesus if we are to find God. So what does this look like? There are at least four elements that this relationship must have. First of all, our relationship with Christ is one of acceptance. Not only does this mean that we must understand that God, through Jesus, has accepted us as sons rather than slaves, but that we must also accept Christ for Who He Is. This was the mistake of the Pharisees. Like the man who bases his attraction in women entirely on the distorted media portrayal of the "perfect woman[73]," the Pharisees created for themselves an image of the Messiah and missed the Christ.

We must acknowledge the uniqueness of the real Christ. We affirm that He was who He said He was. Jesus made some bold claims in His life. He said that He and the Father were One Essence. He claimed that He could forgive sins. He said that no one could come to God except through Him. He claimed to be YHWH

---

[73]   In many ways, the way the media portrays that elusive "perfect woman" is the way the Pharisees were looking for the Christ. They had all sorts of Botox-injected expectations of the Messiah that would ultimately prevent them from meeting the real thing when He was literally staring them in the face.

Himself. Jesus made some claims that require our response simply because of the astounding boldness, weight, and impact.

In today's society, it is very popular to think of Jesus as a "good moral teacher." Many people place Jesus in the same category as they do Gandhi, Winston Churchill, or perhaps Socrates. They see Him as a good person who taught good things that should be followed to some degree. The fastest growing religion in the world today, Islam, even views Jesus as the "perfect prophet," second (by a great distance, mind you) only to Muhammad. The problem, though, is that Jesus didn't leave us with such an option.

Jesus cannot simply be a good moral teacher considering the claims he made. The legen[74]dary C. S. Lewis summed up this point by saying that Christ was either one of three things. He was either a liar, a lunatic (in the same vein as one who thinks that they are a glass of orange juice), or He was who He said He was. Jesus claimed to be God eternal. He claimed that no one could be saved except through Him. He did not leave Himself open to be a good moral teacher, or just a prophet.

As Lewis points out, if Jesus was not correct in saying that He is God, then He was either lying to us, which would eliminate His right to be a good moral teacher, or He was absolutely bonkers. Either way, if Jesus was not Who He said He was, then He simply cannot be considered good. Jesus did not leave us with an option in how we would regard Him other than Lord, lunatic, or liar[75].

If we affirm the above and believe that Jesus was exactly who He claimed to be, then we must give Him our trust and faith. Biblical faith is not the same as what we call "blind faith" in today's society. Biblical faith was an informed faith. It meant that there was some knowledge. On the other hand, there is the element of faith that is "believing in what we do not see" (Hebrews 11:1).

---

[74] Wait for it…

[75] Lewis, 52.

Both elements are present in Biblical faith. We have knowledge of many things that Jesus told us through His Word. We are able to have a faith based on knowledge in these areas. However, there are many things that we must take God's (and the Gospel writers') word on.

The chief of these is the resurrection of Jesus the Christ in His physical body after being crucified and dead for three days. This element we must take in the "believing what we do not see" sense. None of us were present to witness the resurrected Christ, however we must believe in this or our faith is baseless and will die. In the book of Romans, Paul tells us that we must "confess with our mouth Jesus as Lord, and believe in our hearts that God raised Him from the dead.[76]"

Why is this so important? If Jesus Christ did not physically resurrect from the dead, we would still be dead in our sins. Because He is alive, He is capable of being known and related to as living. Many great religions have savior-like figures that have died. The difference between the true faith and all of the imposters is that Jesus the Christ rose and lives. We alone serve a God Who is able to be called the Living God.

Christ alone is able to save us. Religion is not. Religion is a dead list of things we try to do to earn salvation. "Saving faith," as Dr. Charles Lake points out, "is that act by which I transfer my faith from trusting in my own efforts for salvation and deposit it in what He has done on Calvary." Ephesians 2:8-9 paints the best picture of this. The problem that the Pharisees faced, and every other "religion" in the world today faces, is that something must be done for salvation to be "earned." Ephesians 2:8-9 tells us that we have been saved by the grace of God alone through faith alone. It is not a result of any "good deed" we could produce, so no one can boast that they've somehow figured out how to be "good enough" to make it.

---

[76] Romans 10:9

Once we have a grasp on these two concepts, we then move into the third element of the basis of our relationship with Christ. The third element is that of confession. We must openly and unashamedly confess Christ before others. In Romans 1:16, Paul says, "For I am not ashamed of the gospel, for it is the power of God for salvation to everyone who believes..." This unashamed proclamation is a direct by-product of a true and vibrant faith in and acceptance of Christ.

Think about the last dating relationship you entered into. More than likely, the first thing you did after he/she said "yes" was to go out and brag about it to your friends and mockers alike. The same fervor should follow our entrance into a relationship with the Messiah. In fact, Jesus says in Matthew 10:32-33 that anyone who denies Christ before men will also be denied by Christ before God. This is similar to the scenario of a man who gets married, but refuses to wear his wedding ring. If he is ashamed to proclaim his bride to the world, well, let's just say there are likely to be consequences.

The final piece in the basis of our relationship with Christ is that of assurance. It's not enough to think or hope that Christ is who He says He is, we have to know for sure that what we believe is true (when tempered on the correct foundation of God's Character, of course). When we do this, we come to know even ourselves better than before. God's love transforms us.

No longer are we slaves to a religion of pointless rules like the Pharisees were, we are now sons and daughters of God. Romans 8:15-16 tells us that "[we] have not received a spirit of slavery leading to fear again, but [we] have received a spirit of adoption by which we cry out, 'Abba! Father!'" Just as we discovered in lesson two, Jesus broke the mold by telling us that we can come before God with confidence as His children and relate to Him as Dada.

Now that we understand the basis of our relationship, we need to discuss how we maintain this relationship. It's critical for you to understand that there is still nothing you can do to earn salvation or your place as God's child. That is furthest from the truth.

However, if this is really a relationship, it should look something like a relationship. You can't have a relationship without certain elements present. You can't have a relationship without some effort. Often times, this means that you must actively do certain things, not to "earn" the relationship, but to maintain it and help it grow stronger.

Think about the human relationships we focus on every day. I, for example, am a married man. I claim to have a relationship with my wife. Imagine with me for a moment if I proudly proclaimed to others that I am married, and yet, my wife and I only spoke to each other once a week for about an hour. What if, I actually spent most of my time flirting with other girls and did all I could to avoid any direct ties to my wife? Would you say that I, in truth, had a relationship with my wife[77]? I would think not.

We humans pride ourselves on being able to figure out what it takes to make relationships work[78] and yet we never think to apply these same insights to our "relationship" with Christ. Just as a human relationship is maintained by time spent together, seeking knowledge of one another, an entrance into a relationship with one another's family and friends, and (eventually) some form of ultimate commitment, these same elements help us to maintain our relationship with Jesus.

Mutual association helps maintain our relationship with Christ. As with your boyfriend/girlfriend or husband/wife, you cannot claim a healthy relationship with Christ and spend no time with Him. If you're not coming before Him daily, your relationship will stagnate. This is why we talked earlier about having a devotion time of at least 15 minutes a day. We claim that this is the most important relationship in our lives and yet do not even spend 15 minutes a day

---

[77] I, in truth, would likely have a frying pan alongside my head…

[78] Just look at all the self-help and romance novels that get sold. I'm telling you, Fabio is still selling pictures of himself to book companies as you read this.

together? Try that on your wife or kids and see how your relationship ends up after a short time. I highly doubt your wife will put up with that for very long.

There must also be an element of communication. Just as communication is essential in a human relationship, we can't expect a strong bond with God if we are not communicating with Him. Think about how much time you spend communicating with your significant other, especially early on in the relationship. More than likely, communication is a big deal in your relationship. If not, you may need to focus your efforts back into that relationship, as well.

There are so many benefits from time spent in communication with God that I couldn't even begin to list them all here. The focus, however, is that we are simply allowed to come before our Dada. We are allowed to do something that the Pharisees of Jesus' day may have found heretical...we are allowed to relate to God as a personal friend. We are allowed to come before our Father. We do not have to fear, but are allowed to come before God with confidence.

That's huge, but do we really feel the impact of it? My son is about ten months old as I write this. My wife tells me that each day around the time I come home from work, Logan crawls over to the front door, begins patting it, and repeating "dada...dada..." over and over. He knows I'm coming home. He's excited to see me and spend time with me. When I open the door, his face lights up in a way that melts my heart every single time. That's the type of relationship God offers to us.

A third area of relationship that must be maintained is obedience. Again, this does not earn us our salvation. That's not the point. That's the point of "religion," perhaps, but the point of a relationship is love. Imagine again your significant other. After some short time you likely found that there are some do's and don'ts that this person placed into your relationship. Some are more obvious and universal than others. You would not expect to maintain your relationship and break the rule of violating their trust with another person, for example. That one is pretty easy. It takes time to learn that they also don't want you spitting in the sink, leaving your clothes on the floor by your side of the bed, or running the dishwasher while they're in the shower. Those things only come from time together[79].

Just as in our human relationships, our relationship with Christ should be consumed by, in love, doing what He has told us to do. This is just a part of a healthy relationship. If we truly love God, far from doing works to try to earn His favor, we should be compelled by His love into obedience. This is why John was able to say in 1 John 5:3-4, "for this is the love of God, that we keep His commandments; and His commandments are not burdensome. For whatever is born of God overcomes the world; and this is the victory that has overcome the world—our faith."

If you really understand God as a God of holiness and love, consistent with the image of Father, and having our best interests at heart, this shouldn't be a sticking point in your relationship with Him. Who wouldn't want to obey such a God? If you know He only wants good things for you, that He knows infinitely better than you, and even knows you better than you know yourself, the choice to obey, though not at all easy, becomes obvious. If you find yourself in difficulty with this, then very likely you have not truly come to understand the proper foundation of Who God is, or your sin is still trying to take hold of you. Sin is self-rule. It only seeks its own ends. If you don't feel some increasing degree in comfort in your obedience to Christ (not saying it will be easy), then you need to ask yourself who's behind the steering wheel.

The final element in maintaining your relationship with Christ is found in sharing it. Here is the one area where our analogy to human relationships falls flat on its face. If I were to "give my wife"

---

[79] For example: there's an unspoken rule in my house that I must always bring home chocolate when my wife has had a bad day...even when I don't know in advance that a bad day is being had.

to others, then I would not grow our relationship, but kill it. In contrast to this, if you keep your relationship with Christ to yourself, it will rust into the ground slowly[80]. Christ designed our relationship with Him to be revolutionary in the fact that it will only grow as you give it away.

Picture a river. When it's fed by a greater source and flows to the ends of the earth, it purifies itself. When you stop the flow, infestation begins slowly to take over. It is only in channeling our relationship with Christ to others that it will never become stagnant. This doesn't mean that you should spend every day on the street corners with a bullhorn and a sign that says "repent." It means that as you are discipled, you are called to share what you find in God and give it to others.

You are not entering this discipleship process just so you can look like Jesus, but also so that you can help others start to look more like Him. If you're truly becoming a disciple of Christ, your relationship should become infectious and you should begin to share that discipleship process with others. It's sort of like when you have a favorite sports team or favorite movie. You want others to experience the joy and rapture you're experiencing. It's just...Jesus is so much better than sports or movies! So our joy and desire to share Him with others should be proportionately greater than the joy of any sporting event[81] or any movie.

I want to challenge you with one last thought for this lesson. What does your relationship with Christ look like now? What will it look like in six months if you continue the path you're on without making adjustments? Colossians 1:13-20 has a great final insight for this chapter that I want you to consider. In this passage, Paul starts

---

[80] Like those old cars you see on *American Pickers*.

[81] If your love and excitement for the Super Bowl is greater than your joy and excitement about sharing this amazing relationship of love with others... there's a seriously massive crack in your foundation.

out by saying that, "He [Christ] rescued us from the domain of darkness, and transferred us to the kingdom of His beloved Son, in whom we have redemption, the forgiveness of sins." We have all been rescued from the domain of darkness, but some seem to exemplify this more than others.

Though we all have the same opportunity to come to this amazing relationship with Christ, it's a strange fact that though Christ is present in all Christians, He is only prominent in some. Though we all have the Spirit of God in us and are temples for the Holy Spirit Himself, only some display this as a prominent feature in their lives. Why is this? Further, if Christ is present in all Christians and prominent in some, why is He preeminent in only a small few? Don't let this merely be a rhetorical question. What is it that separates the few who seem to be consumed by Christ from the rest of us?

I believe that this lesson holds the answer. Look back over it. Think about what elements a human relationship has and how these often mirror our relationship with God. Then, think about your relationship with Him. What areas look very little like a real relationship? Where have you turned this relationship into a binding and deadly religion? Give yourself one or two measurable and practical goals in each area. Think about what level you want to be committed to Christ in your life. Are you happy with Him merely being present? Or would you rather be consumed whole?

How you answer this question is the only thing that can empower what you'll do to make sure your relationship with Christ is a healthy one. It all comes down to the question, "Who am I going to be in love with?" God is more interested in your being than in your doing. Are you still trying to earn your way to Him? Or have you fallen completely in love with Christ and live obediently as an aspect of your love relationship? The answer to those questions will shape the house you build back on your spiritual foundation.

Donald Miller may have stated it best when he said, "Our 'behavior' will not be changed long with self-discipline (alone), but fall in love and a human will accomplish what he never thought possible…by accepting God's love for us, we fall in love with Him, and only then do we have the fuel we need to obey[82]."

---

[82]   Miller, Donald. *Blue Like Jazz*, Thomas Nelson: Nashville, TN, 2003, 86.

Lesson 5 Assignment Sheet

1. Quiet Time
   a. Daily prayer, reading, and application of God's Word.
   b. Take the lesson learned this week before God and ask Him what's missing, needing focus, etc.

2. Scripture Memorization
   a. Review 2 Corinthians 5:17, 1 John 4:8, Revelation 4:8b, John 15:7-8, Psalm 119:11, Psalm 119:105.
   b. Learn 1 John 5:11-12.

3. Prayer Partnership
   a. Lovingly encourage one another daily.
   b. Meet together once outside of group and pray together.

4. Quiet Time Log
   a. Turn in this week's Quiet Time Log to your disciple-maker for review.
   b. Start a new week.

"And the testimony is this, that God has given us eternal life, and this life is in His Son. He who has the Son has the life; he who does not have the Son of God does not have the life."

1 John 5:11-12 (NASB)

Lesson 6—

Communication with Your Best Friend

Few stories in Scripture are as beloved to people of the Judeo-Christian faith as the story of the Exodus from Egypt. Few lists of important historical figures from these two faith histories would not include God's servant Moses. The life of Moses is a fascinating one. Born under an oppressive ruler, Moses was supposed to be murdered as an infant. Instead, God spared him so dramatically that he became a son to the very tyrant who issued the murderous decree. Given a life of luxury as a prince of Egypt, Moses lived the life of dreams until a fateful skirmish left him a murderer and wanted man.

Fast forward many years and Moses seemingly stumbles upon a burning bush that speaks to him, telling him that he will deliver God's people out from under the hand of Pharaoh. Moses' response that he was slow of speech did not hinder "I Am That I Am" from sending Moses to be the vessel of deliverance to the Hebrew people. Then comes the fun parts; plagues of frogs and locusts, boils, water turning to blood, and the death of the firstborn sons in an event that came to be called the Passover.

The story of the Exodus is one of the few stories every generation seems to be inspired to share with their children. Whether through Hollywood blockbusters such as *The Ten Commandments* and *The Prince of Egypt*, or simple children's Sunday school lessons, Moses is a central figure in the life of our faith. He is even given the honor of being listed in the "Hall of Faith" in Hebrews chapter 11 as a shining example of a man who walked with God[83]. Perhaps most honoring of all, though, is the fact that Moses shows up on a mountain with Elijah before a transfigured Christ, a short while before Jesus' death.

Looking at this list, Moses has a lot of spiritual cred to his name. However, possibly the single most honoring statement about Moses is inscribed in Exodus 33:11. This verse says, "Thus the Lord used to speak to Moses face to face, just as a man speaks to his friend." How do you top that? What more could a disciple of Christ possibly seek than speaking face to face with God as a friend?

Here's the clincher; now that Christ has sent His Spirit to live with us, we are able to come before God as His friends. Remember John 15:15 from the last lesson? Jesus told us that He no longer calls us servants or slaves, but friends. We are called friends of a holy God of love. While we may not be able to come before God face to face in a physical sense as Moses may have, we are able to meet Him spirit to Spirit through the Helper that He left with us.

As you were reminded in the last lesson, communication is an important aspect of our relationship with God. The problem is that we're terrible at communication. Breakdown in communication is the single most selected answer when something goes wrong in relationships. Why do you think that is? What are we missing? If we are tasked to have effective communication in both human relationships and in our relationship with God, why are we so bad at it?

Let me ask you another question to begin to answer this dilemma. What are the fewest elements you can have and still have fellowship and effective communication with one another? Think about that

---

[83] The closest most people get to this nowadays is stalking Morgan Freeman. Which is something I know nothing about, of course.

for a second. While you're thinking, let's take a look at 1 John 1:3 (NASB). "What we have seen and heard we proclaim to you also, so that you too may have fellowship with us; and indeed our fellowship is with the Father, and with His Son Jesus Christ."

Ok, time's up. The fewest elements you can have in conversation are: you talk to me and I listen, and I talk to you and you listen. That's it. That's the most basic form. Unfortunately, there's so much more than the basics we have to consider. Our problem is that too many of us follow an example of poor communication with God, even in prayer. An example of poor communication with God would look like this: we talk to God and then stop, walk away, and/or move on. In another setting, God's Word speaks to us. We give it an approving nod, but then file those thoughts away as we think about where we're going for lunch.

Though this may summarize the minimum number of elements needed for communication and fellowship, it does not exemplify effective communication. In an example of effective communication, we would communicate back to God in prayer what He is already speaking to us. All the while, God's Word then encourages our prayer for others. Then, the cycle begins again. In the first example, there was nothing more than one-sided speaking. It doesn't matter if this is from God to us, or from us to God. Prayer should rarely, if ever, be one-sided, and if there is an instance where this is the case, God should be the One speaking. In the second example, there is a life transference and deeper understanding that is fostered. Sadly, this is not the model most Christians follow in their conversations with The Most High.

The Biblical model for prayer is communication in reciprocation. Psalm 27:8 models this when it says, "When You said, 'seek My face,' my heart said to You, 'Your face, O Lord, I shall seek.'" Isn't that a great prayer? Isn't that a powerful statement? On the average, however, our prayer looks more like a grocery list we made while we were very hungry[84]. Rarely do we come before God in humble submission and reverence. Rather, we tend to come to Christ like we came to Santa Clause's lap when we were children. We state our needs in a rather demanding manner, get our picture taken (mostly as evidence that we gave our list to him and can, therefore, kick and scream if we don't get what we want), and then stamp our feet and hold our breath as we await the demands we placed upon Him.

Despite knowing better, my prayers before bed often comprise little more than a ransom letter to God asking for my immediate demands[85]. That is, if I make it that far before I drift slowly into Neverland. Luckily, at least luckily for me, prayers presented to God when I'm alert don't typically follow this slumber-induced pattern. Do you agree with me, though, that most of our prayers, even as devoted children of God, break down into something like this?

In truth, the pattern that typically presents itself in our "communication" with God goes a little like this: First of all, we come across a problem in our life or in the life of someone we care about. This problem is allowed to fester in our minds for some time and is finally taken before God. Our prayer may then start out, "Heavenly Father," but that is the last reference to God we make other than honestly seeking His immediate attention to whatever huge issue or problem is before us. We then state our case as to why this person needs _____, or why this situation must _____, and restate it again just in case He didn't hear it or

---

[84] Ineffective prayer, example 1: While bowing my head to pray before a meal, I once said to God, "Thank you for calling Sears, this is Lee, how may I help you?"

[85] Ineffective prayer, example 2: My buddy Mike Weeks sat down at our college lunch table, bowed his head, and audibly started counting. Once our snickering grew loud enough, he finally realized what he was doing. Mike had had a long day.

was somehow distracted by someone else's prayers. If we have any spiritual energy left, we may add one or two more elements to the prayer, but more than likely this supplication (meaning "request") will immediately follow a frantic "Amen."

We walk away from this prayer with very little peace in our hearts and then immediately begin to wonder why. After all, didn't the Bible tell us that "the peace of God which surpasses all comprehension" would "guard our hearts and (our) minds in Christ Jesus" (Philippians 4:6-7)? So why is there so little peace after this prayer[86]? Is it any wonder that even the disciples came to Christ directly and asked Him to teach them (and us) how to pray?

Luckily for us, their request was granted. In the book of Acts[87], after having asked Jesus to show them how to pray, the disciples seem to finally get it right. Some have said that the book of Acts, which is short for "The Acts of the Apostles," could also be called "The Acts of Prayer." So much of the book of Acts is a testament to the power of proper prayer that it becomes a dominant theme throughout that book. Suddenly these once-timid disciples, who asked Jesus to teach them how to pray, are praying these earth-shattering prayers that changed the course of history as we know it.

We are often told that we should pray and given no instructions to make that happen. More than likely, the way you learned how to pray was from watching someone else do it or, in rare cases, seeing it done on TV. For the moment, I'm not talking about that deep life transference, but a scenario where you watched a pastor or church leader pray in public once, or saw grandpa pray at dinner, and then

---

[86] Ineffective prayer, example 3: When I was little, I thought that if I opened my eyes at any time during the prayer, it didn't count. As soon as I opened my eyes, I would have to start the whole prayer over again.

[87] Acts follows the four Gospels and is a direct follow up to the Gospel of Luke, specifically.

modeled all of your prayers after that[88]. In this scenario, many of us have actually been "shown" how to pray by someone who was, themselves, never shown how to pray, if we're even shown at all.

The bulk of this lesson will be in teaching you how to pray. Just as there are several different and valid ways that you can study the Bible, there are several different methods of prayer. Because of this, there is no way we will be able to discuss them all here. So for our lesson, we're going to look at the prayer Jesus taught His disciples in Matthew chapter six. Before you continue in this lesson, I encourage you to take out your Bible and read Matthew 6:5-15. I ask you to read this from your own Bible, rather than printing it here in order to reinforce the habit of getting you into your own personal Bible more. As you read though this passage, don't be afraid to mark what you're reading and make comments on any insights that you glean. I'll give you time to read that passage now.

Now that you've read Jesus' words on prayer, allow me to point you toward some insights. Let's first look at verse nine. In this verse, Jesus tells us that we are to "pray, then, in this way." Does Jesus mean that we can only pray The Lord's Prayer word for word and never anything else? No. In fact, the Lord's Prayer itself can become the "meaningless repetition" Jesus warned about if we simply go through the motions without thinking about what we're even saying. If you're just praying through the Lord's Prayer so you can get done with it or are checked out mentally and spiritually but mouthing the words… you've turned it into meaningless repetition.

When Jesus says to "pray, then, in this way," He is not giving you a word for word script that you must follow (though praying the Lord's Prayer with the right heart is a very powerful way to

---

[88] Ineffective prayer, example 4: At Wrestlemania 6, the Ultimate Warrior said "Hulk Hogan" every other word while cutting a promo on him. Ever since then, I've watched countless pastors do the same thing, only using the words "Father God," and sweating and snorting marginally less.

communicate with God), but rather a grouping of elements that should be included in true and vibrant prayer. What Jesus says is powerful. For a moment, then, let's dissect this, remembering that such a dissection is only half of the equation that includes allowing the words of the Word to speak over us and allowing the insights application into our lives.

"Our Father Who is in Heaven, hallowed be Your Name. Your kingdom come, Your will be done, on earth as it is in heaven." The first element of Jesus' prayer is an acknowledgement of Who God is and submission to His character (Name). Jesus didn't start out, "Ok God, I need _____.[89]" Instead, He first recognized Who God is. And, what He says is remarkable. First, He refers to God as Father. Remember that, in this day and age, this was a revolutionary way to relate to God. Second, He recognizes God's kingdom. In just this short phrase you come to an understanding of both God's immanence (in heaven) and His transcendence (Father). That's huge.

Next, He reminds us of God's holiness. "Hallowed be Your Name," is a reminder of how holy God's Character is. Here again, we are presented with a God of Love (Father) who is Holy (Hallowed). This works right back into Lesson 2 and the need for a proper foundation[90]. This prayer has all of that built into the very first sentence! In prayer, we need to recognize and remind ourselves exactly Who we're praying to before anything else!

"Your Kingdom come, Your will be done, on earth as it is in heaven." The next element of the prayer is a sort of confession of how small we are and a vow of submission to a huge God. Human beings spend so much of their lives trying to puff themselves up living in their own will and creating their own kingdoms. We even

---

[89] Ah, the endless fun had with fill-in-the-blanks. First thing that comes to mind for me was a pony on this one. Couldn't begin to tell you why.

[90] Jesus' foundation was pretty solid, I hear.

say "a man's home is his castle." We have kingdom language built into the most basic references we use for ourselves...but it's the wrong kingdom. Jesus reminds us that we are nothing before God and that His Kingdom and His will are the point. He asks us, so subtly, to give up our striving after our own kingdom and focus on the kingdom of God and the will of God and that it be brought to earth.

"Give us this day our daily bread." Here, we humble ourselves further by admitting our need of God's supply. Here we see Jesus telling us not to ask God for the world, but only for our daily needs. He knows, as the Bible also teaches in other places, that having more than what we need can draw our hearts away from God. So, He teaches us to ask, in humility, only for what we need for that specific day. This is in stark contrast to our many prayers to make us rich and comfortable. How often have we prayed to God for what should be enough to satisfy us for years, rather than just the day ahead of us[91]?

"Forgive us our debts, as we have forgiven our debtors." Here is where Jesus introduces to us that our prayers, though between a Holy God and us, have an effect on others as well as ourselves. Verse 14 and 15 really bring this into focus. We cannot come before God and hold anything against another person. If we do, God will not hear our prayers. Think about that one for a second. God will not hear your prayers if there is a lack of forgiveness in your heart. If we do not forgive others, God will not forgive us. This is just another aspect of that love relationship we have with God. If we are truly in a relationship with I AM, then love and forgiveness

---

[91] Ineffective prayer, example 5: Though I'm not proud of it, I ate at a Hooters restaurant as a teenager. Being the "spiritual one" (you know, at Hooters), my friends gave me the charge to pray. My first words were, "Dear God, please breast this food..." That was the beginning and end of the prayer, as my friends couldn't stop laughing after that.

should flow from us, just as it does from the Source of our love. If we fail to give love and forgiveness (or even just trickle it out to start), our foundation is cracked and we need to re-examine our relationship with God.

"Lead us not into temptation, but deliver us from the evil one." Jesus reminds us that we are a world at war. Jesus didn't say to ignore the problem of evil in the world. He didn't say to hide the fact that temptations will come our way; He simply asked that we pray to God for deliverance from these inevitable temptations.

Look again at the prayer Jesus modeled. There is so much power packed into that prayer, it's no wonder it's considered by many to be the best prayer ever[92]. The fact is, if Jesus said we should pray in this manner, then that is probably what we should do. As a quick aside, I challenge you at some point in your walk of faith to take a look at the prayers Jesus prayed to the Father Himself. Before the pending cross He declared, "Your Kingdom come, Your will be done." While hanging on the cross, seeing the soldiers mock Him and cast lots for His clothes, He declared, "Forgive us our trespasses, as we forgive those who trespass against us."

It shouldn't surprise you to see that though Jesus never again used the exact words of His prayer in Matthew 6, He followed the very advice He modeled to us. Our prayers should look more like Jesus' prayer than a ransom note with a list of demands. So, how do we practically do this?

As mentioned, one way is to use the ACTS method of prayer. Just as the book of Acts is a great place to see the power of prayer, the ACTS method of prayer provides a great, easy to remember, plan for coming before the throne of God. ACTS, of course, is an acronym. Each letter stands for a word that starts with the same letter to make it more memorable. Let's take it one word at a time,

---

[92] Or as Comic Book Guy from *The Simpsons* would say; "Best...Prayer... Ever."

then, and look at what a prayer that follows after Jesus' great prayer could look something like.

The first element in the ACTS method of prayer is Adoration. Just as Jesus started out His prayer, "Our Father in heaven," we should begin our prayers by telling God how great He is. This may sound a bit odd or seem like God is a bit of a megalomaniac, but there is a purpose behind this. Think back to how the "average" prayer started. Most prayers begin with the focus of our mental framework zooming in on whatever the problem at hand is. When you're focused in on the problem, you can't see God for Who He Is. Though the problem could never be bigger than God, we allow it to block Him from our vision.

When you start your prayer by adoring God for how great He is, the whole rest of the prayer starts to shift into a proper focus and the problem isn't blocking your view of God. The problem or need is no longer the biggest thing on your heart. Instead our focus is back on God, Who is able to do "far more abundantly beyond all that we ask or think[93]". Adoring God, then, is not a strange boost to God's ego, but a way in which we remind ourselves just Who we're dealing with. Adoration is the act of loving God for Who He Is. This should always be the framework we create for the rest of our prayer. Truly, when this is the first step before the throne, the rest of the prayer should begin to fall into place better on its own.

When you begin by admitting and reminding yourself of how great God is, the immediate result is to see just how small you are. Far from being a bad thing, this continues to put your prayer in proper perspective. This reminder of God's loving character of holiness should lead you to recognize your smallness before God and repent of your missteps. This is the C in the acronym; Confession.

Confession means "to say the same thing." When you confess something, you literally call it what it is and see it as God sees it.

[93] Ephesians 3:20

You are openly uncovering your sin before God and admitting your dependence on Him. David modeled this to us in Psalm 32:5a, where he said, "I acknowledged my sin to You, and my iniquity I did not hide; I said, 'I will confess my transgressions to the Lord.'"

Let me be precise in this; you are not giving God generalities here. When I was a child, I used to pray, "God forgive me for everything I did wrong today[94]." But isn't there something wrong with this kind of prayer? Sure seems to cover the bases, right? Confession means getting specific before God. It means entering into the guilt of your sin before Him and calling it what it is. It means naming what you've done. When you've lied, it means calling it a lie. When you've lusted, it means calling it adultery. This is not confession before a priest in order to relieve guilt. This is admitting before the High Priest what you've done and how it has affected your relationship with Him. Once it's all out there in the open, all honest and accounted for, your relationship with God will grow. God forgives us of our trespasses.

Admitting with an honest heart the specific sins you've committed against God and man is not a sadistic form of punishment. In fact, doing this is the very thing God uses to free you from the power those sins hold over you. Though you are forgiven from the guilt of sin, until you admit it before God and see how you've broken His heart, you are still likely to give that sin power over you when it attempts to tempt you again. Once you confess it before God and both of your hearts break over it, you will not likely allow that sin to come between you again.

Just as adoration frames your prayer by reminding you how great God is, confession reminds you of how small you, in fact, are. Psalm

---

[94] Ineffective prayer, example 6: I also used to pray that God would help set me up so I wouldn't be a virgin anymore. Apparently I had enough sense to pray, but not enough sense to know the sort of prayer God would honor.

103 reminds us that we are but dust[95]. These two elements shape our prayer and begin to remind us just Who we are praying to and just who we are. The next element has to do with remembering just how God has been with us in the past. Thanksgiving is the T in the ACTS acronym. When we first remember Who God is and how He has been continually faithful to us in life, despite the many legions of ways we continue to break His heart, we should be compelled to thanksgiving. In fact, thanksgiving is almost too little to express the amazing wonder of God's faithfulness to unfaithful creatures.

Thanksgiving is gratitude for the things He has done in our lives, in the world, and in the lives of those around us. When we remember what we deserve in our confession to God, our thanksgiving to Him grows. Because of our sin, we deserve the unrestrained wrath of a holy God, yet He shows us love without measure instead. How could that not cause us to well up with gratitude? But, it's not even just that. In addition to forgiveness and grace, God comes through for us over and over again in so many other areas of our lives!

After we have seen how great God is, how small and sinful we are, and how bountifully He has blessed us, only then are we in the proper frame of mind to ask God for what we need. When we pray in this manner, we've taken that lens in our minds that was fixated on a problem (thereby making it look impassible to us) and pulled the camera back to see the bigger picture. Suddenly, that great need that would have otherwise consumed us now seems so small and insignificant before a God who has our best interests at heart and Who has come through for us time and time again.

God is so big that He created everything, yet so loving that He cares about whatever you have on your heart. Put in proper context, we can begin to see that He has always taken care of our needs, and we need not pray a prayer of lifeless petition, but recognize our Dada

---

[95] There's a funny story about a little kid thinking the preacher said "butt dust," but it's too long for a footnote. Maybe another time?

and how amazingly abundantly giving He truly is. I promise you, if you pray "in this manner" and follow the model of Christ, your prayer life will no longer seem lifeless and stale. Your needs will no longer seem like the most pressing matter in the conversation. Most importantly, your relationship with God will no longer seem quite so one-sided. Perhaps from there we can truly begin to stop telling your God how big your problems are and start telling your problems how big your God is!

Prayer is a commitment, but it is also a privilege that we are able to come before the Creator. To conclude this lesson, I would like to share some insights that were gleaned from Dr. Charles Lake. You'll see many of these echoed back in Jesus' words in Matthew 6. Here, then, are some practical suggestions to finish off your understanding of how to pray.

1. Length does not determine value (Matthew 6:7).
2. Effective prayer comes from a humble heart (Luke 18:9-14).
3. Pray specific prayers for specific answers (John 16:24).
4. Pray Scripturally according to God's Word and will (John 15:7).
5. Pray in faith, with thanksgiving (Philippians 4:6)
6. Don't give up (Luke 11:8)!

Lesson 6 Assignment Sheet

1. Daily Quiet Time
    a. Daily prayer, reading, and application of God's Word.
    b. This week, ask yourself, "How is my prayer time?"
    c. Begin putting this week's lesson into practice.
    d. Begin praying on your knees at your chair as a symbol of your submission before God.

2. Scripture memorization
    a. Review 2 Corinthians 5:17, 1 John 4:8, Revelation 4:8b, John 15:7-8, Psalm 119:11, Psalm 119:105, 1 John 5:11-12.
    b. Learn John 16:24.

3. Prayer partnership
    a. Lovingly remind each other through the week to keep at it and be consistent.
    b. Pray together once outside of group time.

4. Quiet Time Log
    a. Submit your QTL to your disciple-maker for review.
    b. Look back over the notes made by your disciple-maker.

"Until now you have asked nothing in My name. Ask, and you will receive, that your joy may be full."

John 16:24 (ESV)

Lesson 7—

Dealing with Temptation

Very recently during a Men's Fraternity meeting,[96] a discussion was presented about the temptation of Jesus from Luke chapter 4. To set up the story, Jesus has just been baptized by John the Baptist and is about to start His "formal" ministry. Immediately after the baptism, Jesus is "led by the Spirit" into the wilderness. We are then told two things. First, we're told that Jesus fasted for forty days. Second, we're told that the devil came to tempt Him.

One of the many faults I have shading my understanding of the Bible is that I often process exclusively with my brain and very little with my emotions. So, despite being very familiar with the text, our discussion that morning led to some insights that had not hit home with me before. The text itself seems to glance over some huge emotional elements that really shape the understanding we should have of the temptation of Christ.

First of all, the text lets us know that Jesus is sent into the wilderness alone for forty days. I'm an extrovert through and through. My wife, on the other hand, is very much an introvert. Time alone (to a certain degree) drains the fire out of me and can lead to a downcast spirit. For my wife, however, time alone is what she needs to recharge her batteries. From the Scriptures we can see both extroverted and introverted tendencies in the life of Jesus.

---

[96] At the unholy hour of 5 a.m.

In either case, I don't care if Jesus was primarily an extrovert or primarily an introvert…forty days spent completely alone can make a person go just short of crazy.

In 2010, the U. S. saw a major ice storm that effected a large portion of the nation for almost two weeks in a row. After that many days cooped up in the same place, I began to feel my spirit tell me it was caged and needed free. Imagine, now, spending forty days in such a situation, but also cut off from all forms of human interaction. No T.V., no Internet, no blogging, no Facebook, no cell phone, nothing. Forty days of complete and utter solitude.

That's not the only thing the text tells us was going on. It also says that Jesus fasted for these forty days. Fasting means you're not eating, so Jesus had had forty days without human interaction or a cheeseburger[97]. All the text says at this point is that, "He became hungry." No joke. While I am by no means an expert on fasting, my wife and I once engaged in a fast lasting for roughly 14 days. Let me tell you, the first several days of the fast were great. Our bodies, no longer bombarded by chemically altered foods and "food-like-products", were able to begin to heal us in ways that we were not allowing them to for many years. But, then, day 11 happened. After a dozen or so days without food, your body begins to wonder what's going on. It begins to reserve energy and "asks" you not to do all that much. After the 11 to 12 day mark, you want a nap[98].

My wife and I found it hard to stop eating for 14 days and Jesus was on day 40! Just imagine for yourself how ravenous He must have been! Add to that the fact that He was lonely, extremely tired,

---

[97] After a deep search through my Biblical encyclopedia, I must note that apparently they didn't have cheeseburgers in Jesus' days. So, technically, Jesus had gone like 30 years without a cheeseburger.

[98] In fact, you want a Jim Gaffigan-sized nap. By the way, Jim Gaffigan also likes cheeseburgers.

and…that's just the tip of the iceberg of what we know was going on as we come into this temptation story. This is the emotional setting we need to understand when we come to the temptation of Christ. When we see the story through this lens, it begins to make so much sense why satan tempts Jesus with food, power, and a number of other things. Anyone else but Jesus would have probably given up at the mere mention of bread[99] in that emotional state.

The goal of this lesson is to discuss the true nature of temptation and to provide some insights and tools for help in dealing with temptation effectively. I want you to know up front that this is a fairly long session. Be sure to plan adequate time to go over what is here. If you need to, you may wish to stretch a portion of this into your next disciple group meeting, as well.

As we begin, I want you to take a moment to yourself and try to define "temptation." What does it mean? What is it? Take your best educated guess and write it down in the margin and share it with your discipleship group. What did you come up with? Perhaps two quotes by some wonderfully great Christian thinkers will help you along the way. "I cannot control the birds that fly over my head, but I can keep them from making a nest in my hat[100]." These words, penned by the immortal John Wesley, may give some insight. The second quote, penned by my personal favorite thinker, will help us cut directly to the core of any potential misconceptions. As C. S. Lewis states:

---

[99] Or a cheeseburger! Speaking of which, I was once in line at a fast food restaurant and the lady in front of me ordered a cheeseburger without the cheese. The cashier tried, for a couple minutes, to explain that a hamburger *was* a cheeseburger without cheese (and cost less). The woman got really indignant and said something like, "are you going to take my order or not?"

[100] This quote has been alternately attributed to both Martin Luther and John Wesley.

> A silly idea is current that good people do not know what
> temptation means. This is an obvious lie. Only those who
> try to resist temptation know how strong it is...A man
> who gives into temptation after five minutes simply does
> not know what it would have been like an hour later. That
> is why bad people, in one sense, know very little about
> badness. They have lived a very sheltered life by always
> giving in to it[101].

So what is temptation? Temptation is an invitation or enticement
to do evil by offering some apparent advantage. Think or look back
over the temptation of Christ. Satan's attacks were all enticements
to do what would have been evil for Jesus to do by offering Him
what seemed to be an advantage of some sort at face value. The
devil has been around quite a while. Far from being omniscient as
God Himself is, satan has no insight into our own souls. That said,
because he has been around humanity since (quite literally) the dawn
of time, he does have some very tried and true methods of getting
people to stray by offering them ways to do wrong and gain some
apparent advantage from it[102].

The Bible gives us a pretty clear picture of what temptation
is and is not. Take a moment and read James 1:13-15 from your
own Bible. Go ahead, I'll wait for you. James 1:13-15 outlines a
progression of temptation. It first silences any argument that God
tempts us in any way, shape, or form. God does not tempt anyone,
lest you are prone to fall into this theological pitfall. As we discussed
in the previous sections, the character of God is of keen importance
in our life and our discipleship. We must understand that to tempt

---

[101] Lewis, C. S. *Mere Christianity*, HarperCollins: New York, NY, 1952, reprinted 2001, 142.

[102] If you ever wish to delve deeper into this idea read *The Screwtape Letters*, also by C. S. Lewis.

someone to do evil is out of character with the God that is revealed in the Bible. We have an enemy of our souls. This is not God, however, it is the devil.

Next, James outlines that temptation itself is not a sin. If temptation were a sin, Jesus would be one of the world's biggest sinners, since He was "tempted in all things as we are[103]." This would destroy the very foundation of our faith. Temptation is an enticement to sin, not sin itself. This may be a relief to you if you've felt especially tempted of late. When you're tempted to overindulge, for example, you're not sinning in that moment. Make no mistake, however, that temptation, if not fought against, does lead immediately and undeniably into sin.

Following your own desires in a moment of temptation leads to sin. As James says, after our desire has "conceived," it gives birth to sin. From there, once our sin is "full grown," it gives birth to death. Don't miss the intentional parental/birth language the Bible puts before us. Our giving into temptation is like the human act of getting pregnant. We carry around a new bundle of sin once we give in to temptation. Once we give birth, the child is called death. That's some heavy language. We must make sure our distractions do not lead to our destruction.

So, if temptation, though not sin, can still lead to our spiritual deaths, why are we tempted? There are several layers to this. The first answer is that satan was able to splice a sinful nature into all of humanity in the fall of man in the garden. Take a look back to the Fall in Genesis to see what I'm talking about here. So, the enemy worked sin into God's perfect creatures and made them prone to all manner of imperfections and shortcomings. In light of this game-changing reality, James and Genesis both assert that God allows us to face temptations. He doesn't shelter us from them or remove them

---

[103] Hebrews 4:15

from us. Though He Himself does not present the temptations, He also does not stop them.

James 1:2-4 says, "Consider it all joy, my brethren, when encounter various trials, knowing that the testing of your faith produces endurance. And let endurance have its perfect result, so that you may be perfect and complete, lacking in nothing." God doesn't allow temptation to make us sin, but to make us strong! James, among other places in Scripture, lets us know that our faith grows through such trials. Without them, we would not become complete and mature followers of Jesus Christ. In that regard, temptations have a positive effect on our lives. Just like in so many other areas of life, what the devil intended for our destruction, God uses for our deliverance.

That doesn't mean that temptation is good, but it can produce good results if we learn to overcome it. So how do we overcome temptation? Let's jump back to Jesus' time in the wilderness and look at how He overcame a period of tremendous temptation. Here we turn to Luke 4:1-13. I recommend putting this down and reading it from your personal Bible now. Be sure to take a moment to meditate on it, and mark it as you find insights and applications for your own life.

Three things stand out from this section of text: First of all, Jesus knew He could make a conscious choice of what to hunger for (v2-4). When satan tempted Jesus with food, He responded that His food was God's Word. When we "hunger" after a temptation to sin, we need to understand that it is a "hunger" for something that will not and cannot satisfy us. Even when we feast on the sin that that temptation leads to, we will hunger again. The thing about sin is that it will never be full by feeding it. The more you "eat," the more and more hungry sin will get. This is why the Bible says that it gives birth to death. We literally "eat" ourselves to spiritual ruin when we feed sin.

We must make a conscious choice to hunger for what really will satisfy us. This is hard. No one understands this better than the person who is on a diet. That person must choose to hunger for the right kinds of foods or risk losing their willpower and dive deeper into their problem. The same goes for us. We must do as Jesus did and call out and recognize what it is we should be hungering for. We need to hunger for righteousness. We need to hunger for what will truly fill us and satisfy us to the point where we won't need that cheap imitation any longer.

Secondly, Jesus countered each attack by using God's Word. In each one He countered, "It is written." This is another reason we need to hide God's Word in our hearts. God's Word, as it describes itself, is a sword that can be used to cut through our temptations and divide truth from error. We cannot wield this sword if we don't memorize and meditate on God's Word. Jesus was able to counter the devil with Scripture (even when the devil tried to trick Him by misusing the Scripture itself!) and yet we don't see in the text that He had to stop the conversation to look anything up. If we're going to be armed against temptation, we must hide God's Word in our hearts and sharpen that sword every day.

Lastly, we see from the Temptation of Christ that Jesus gave the devil no opportunity. Elsewhere in Scripture it tells us that the devil only needs a little tiny foothold to take control of our lives. If you've ever been rock climbing (indoors or out) you know that a foothold can quite literally be a pencil-shaving sized indention in a rock that you have to anchor your entire body weight on. This is the imagery the Bible leads us to. If we give the devil even the slightest measure of an inch, he'll become our ruler[104].

So often, we fall into sin because we allow temptation to sit and fester in our lives much too long. From all accounts, Jesus countered every temptation of the devil's immediately. Never once did He sit and consider the temptation and what it could do for Him. We must be the same way. The second...the very instant we recognize we're

---

[104] See what I did there?

91

being tempted to sin we must resist the enemy and counter Him with Scripture. Reminding ourselves through the Word of God hidden in our heart what is right will prevent us from doing what is wrong, but we must do it quickly. If we allow temptation to hang around it will convince us to do what we are already so prone to do and try to justify our pending actions.

Jesus didn't justify anything. He didn't allow a second to pass before He swatted temptation away. "That's all well and good," you may be saying to yourself, "but He had the advantage of being God in the flesh." Think about this for a second. While in some areas we're tempted to downplay the fact that Jesus is God, it is equally dangerous to forget that Jesus was fully man, as well. The fact that He's God in the flesh, if you read through the temptations the deceiver used, actually may have made it harder on Him. Jesus was tempted to do things that were not to be done at that time, but that He, as God, had the power to do. Jesus actually had to show much more restraint than we could ever have mustered.

So maybe here you will say that you understand that, but that, "Jesus could never relate to me personally, since He couldn't have faced what I face in temptation." It is also folly to assume that Jesus only was tempted with a certain breed of temptation that was special to Him. While the latter temptations may have been unique to Jesus, the first temptation was for food. That sounds pretty common to me. The writer of Hebrews silences our arguments in 5:15-16 when he tells us that Christ faced all that we face and so much more. He was tempted in every way we are tempted and in ways we could not possibly understand. So, far from Jesus/God not being able to understand our temptations, He understands them so much better than we can ourselves.

Now we get practical. What do we do when we're tempted? Here you will need to turn to and read 1 Corinthians 10:13 from your own Bible. Pay close attention to this verse. It's also your memory verse for the coming week. 1 Corinthians 10:13 is a powerful tool in staying away from the enticements of sin. This verse teaches us that though we are not all going to face the same exact temptations, we are tempted to the same degree. "All temptation is common to man…"

God won't allow us to take on more than we can handle. God, as it says, is faithful. Though He doesn't prevent temptation itself from happening to us, He does prevent it from getting too big for us. This powerfully shows the Father heart of God. He, like a good parent, allows us to face a degree of evil under our own will, but if it gets to be more than we are able, He steps in and takes our hand. What a wonderful God we have and call "Dada." It's interesting to note that this verse on temptation centers on God's faithfulness.

The way in which God steps in for us is to provide a way out. Think about the last time you were tempted. That may not have been more than an hour ago. When you were enticed to do evil through the offering of some apparent advantage, can you honestly say that you didn't immediately see where the escape hatch was, as well? I know from my own experiences that God will often get my attention in subtle ways when I'm facing temptation. Other times, He's even not so subtle. I'll get a phone call from a leader in my church or something of that nature that clearly speaks to the fact that God is providing an immediate escape hatch.

The wonderful truth is that God is faithful every single time. There's never a moment where God is caught off guard by any temptation that comes before us. He's never busy or using the bathroom, as Elijah proclaimed of other false gods on Mount Carmel. He really is faithful every single time. Take a look at Lamentations 3:22-25 for some more insight into this.

Whatever temptation we face, we must understand that our temptations are all common to man. Our specific temptation is not unique. Whatever problem you face, through Jesus Christ you can overcome it. But, let's get even more practical. It may also help you to understand that there are certain mindsets that leave us more prone to temptation's siren call. In these times, you may need extra prayer and to have your sword ready and sharpened. What I'm talking about are emotional and physical states that make us more prone to the wiles of temptation.

To overcome temptation, you need to learn what H.A.L.T.S. you. All men/women are more prone to sin when they are Hungry, Angry, Lonely, Tired, and Sexually-charged. Think about it, why did your mother tell you never to go to the grocery store when you're hungry[105]? The answer should be obvious. In the same manner, when you're angry (and etc.), you're more prone[106] to fall into sin. Each of these states of being opens us up to temptation and makes it easier to fall into different types or categories of sin. Anger will often lead to more violent and aggressively-natured sins. Loneliness will lead to more internal sins, such as self-mutilation. Of course, when we're sexually charged, we are more prone to sins of lust and adultery.

It doesn't take long to see the truth in this matter. What makes it worse is that these emotional states often go together. When we're hungry, we often feel tired. When we're lonely, we may also be more likely to be sexually charged in the wrong way. When this happens, we need an even stronger devotion to God and even more prayer for His help. It's encouraging to know that the very Jesus that we are calling out to faced several of these states at once when He was tempted by the devil and the way He overcame them is also open to us! He faced all that we face and more.

The final bit of advice on this matter is from James 4:7. In this verse, we sum up what it takes to overcome temptation, and thereby, sin. In this masterful verse, James tells us that we first simply need to submit our whole life to God. If we draw close to God, God will

---

[105] As a male, I'm always hungry…which is why my wife recently banned me from going grocery shopping alone. Somehow, I always blow our budget and then some every time I go to the store.

[106] Since "proner" isn't a real word.

draw close to us. If we memorize and internalize His Word, spend time in prayer with Him, and devote ourselves to Him, He will likewise draw closer to us. This sums up much of what was said above. James also lets us know that if we resist the devil in the power of God, he will flee from us.

That's an amazing promise. To close out this lesson, I will leave you with one more promise to add to your arsenal. It is found in Romans 8:28. "And we know that God causes all things to work together for good to those who love God, to those who are called according to His purpose."

Amen.

Lesson 7 Assignment Sheet

1. Daily Quiet Time
   a. As you do battle with the enemy this week, remember that his ultimate victory is your spiritual defeat. Begin using the Scriptures you have already committed to memory as weapons in your spiritual warfare.

2. Scripture memorization
   a. Review 2 Corinthians 5:17, 1 John 4:8, Revelation 4:8b, John 15:7-8, Psalm 119:11, Psalm 119: 105, 1 John 5:11-12, and John 16:24.
   b. Learn 1 Corinthians 10:13.

3. Prayer partnership
   a. Encourage each other in your battle with temptation. Make each other available to call as a way out if temptation is overcoming you.
   b. Spend some time in accountability with your prayer partner this week.

4. Quiet Time Log
   a. Turn in your QTL to your disciple-maker for review.
   b. Begin a new QTL for the week.

"No temptation has overtaken you that is not common to man. God is faithful, and He will not let you be tempted beyond your ability, but with the temptation He will also provide the way of escape, that you may be able to endure it."

1 Corinthians 10:13 (ESV)

Lesson 8—

The Ministry of the Helper

When I was a child, I dreamt of being a professional wrestler. Nerdy, I know. Back in the 1980's, there was only one man who sat on top of the wrestling world: Hulk Hogan. To most wrestling fans, Hulk still sits atop an elite list as one of the, if not the very, best wrestlers that will ever grace the squared-circle. Growing up, I certainly believed in the power of Hulkamania[107].

Whenever my best friend would come over to hang out, we would pretend we were wrestlers. He was always The Ultimate Warrior and I was always the immortal Hulk Hogan. Suddenly, my room was no longer the place I slept in. Suddenly, it was Madison Square Garden. The walls were no longer hung sheet-rock, they were ropes that we would throw each other against and bounce back into a big boot or a power slam. In my mind (whether it happened this way or not), it would always end the same way with me flying through the air of the imaginary arena and landing the devastating Hogan leg drop to put my "ultimate" friend down for the count.

Fast-forward into my late teens. On what seemed like a whisper, I moved over a thousand miles from Casper, Wyoming

---

[107] Strange fact, but "Real American" can still get me pumped and ready to go. Some days, I use it as my alarm clock ringer when I need to leg drop the world.

to Dallas, Texas and joined the Christian Wrestling Federation[108]. In fact, for a while I even got a chance to live in the home of the owner and founder, Rob Vaughn. Over a period of nine months I received training from an exceptional Indy wrestler, who was himself trained by the legendary Lou Thesz. It was, in some small way, the realization of a childhood dream. I even got to drop an actual Hogan leg drop on my new buddy Phil to close out our first practice "match."

I spent the better part of a year learning what it meant to become those characters that I had dreamed about when I was a kid. My trainer was great at that. At the drop of a hat, he could "take on" the motions and nuanced movements of popular stars at the time, such as "Stone Cold" Steve Austin, "HBK" Shawn Michaels, and The Rock. It was as if he were somehow channeling them, or something.

This got me thinking. What if I could, somehow, have Hulk Hogan get into my head and live right inside my skin? Then I could go from simply imitating this iconic leg drop and signature "Hulk-up" to moving in the exact way Hulk moves. I could think in the exact way that Hulk thinks. In a way, I could somehow become just like him. So what does a story about my childhood dream have to do with discipleship? You may be surprised to find out that it is actually quite a bit.

Up to this point in our discipleship journey, we've really only focused on two-thirds of what Christians commonly call "The Trinity." We've spoken both directly and indirectly about the Father and His Son Jesus Christ, but we have yet to even really mention the Holy Spirit. This is a tragedy, because just like Jesus Himself, the Holy Spirit plays an intimate and immeasurable role in our discipleship.

---

[108] Yup. I can list the "CWF" alongside Liberty Baptist Theological Seminary and Mid-America Christian University as places I've "studied." You could call this one the "school of hard knocks". Too corny?

When I felt that God might be leading me to Texas and opening doors to join a wrestling ministry, I went dreaming of becoming like Hulk Hogan, Goldberg, and The Rock. I felt that if I could be like them, get "inside their heads" so to speak, I could become the next great star in sports entertainment. What I didn't realize was that God was more concerned about making me more like Himself than He was Hulk Hogan. And, despite my attempts to fashion myself after the Hulkster, Jesus sent His Spirit to live inside of me and made His transformative power apparent in a very real way. Rather than concern Himself with making me like someone else, God's Spirit took me on a journey that daily had me look and act more and more like Him.

You can never have Tiger Woods live inside you to make you a better golfer. Michael Jordan cannot transfer his legendary basketball skills to you through a magical pair of sneakers[109]. You can't go to the Hard Rock Café and walk out a Rock and Roll legend from simply eating a burger and taking in the ambiance of the guitars on the wall. However, God has given His Spirit to live inside of you and make you more like Him every single day. Shouldn't that encourage you? As much as I loved the Hulkster, I would rather have the God of the universe's help from within than the power of Hulkamania.

The focus of this lesson will be to reveal the nature of the Holy Spirit. We'll start our journey in John chapter 16. Go ahead and read that chapter in your own Bible for a moment. Have you ever really thought about Who the Holy Spirit is? Depending on your faith background and how "charismatic" that was, you may or may not have. John 16:7 refers to Him as our "comforter" or "helper." The Greek word used is paraclete, which more literally means "One called alongside to help." This is important because Jesus Himself made it very clear that He was "going away." Yet, as He went away, He promised us that He would send a paraclete. Instead of showing

---

[109] Despite what Nike and at least two movies would have you believe.

us the way, but then leaving us to face life in this world alone, Jesus left us with One who comes alongside of us and helps us. Don't let that simple word "help" fool you. I'm not talking about giving you the answers to your math homework[110], I'm talking about God's Spirit coming alongside to save and empower your life.

Have you ever cried out in anguish, "God, help me!" or, "Lord, give me strength!" in the midst of some personal struggle? God has graciously given us SomeOne who comes to our aid. The even greater news, though, is that this Helper comes to us not just in times of trouble, but also in each moment of our lives. In John 16:7, Jesus promised His disciples (and all future disciples) that He would send "the Comforter." He is the third Person of the Holy Trinity, and He is personal with us in our lives.

The Holy Spirit has already been at work in your life in many ways. You may not have recognized them, but Scripture tells us of many roles that the third Person of the Trinity fulfills. First of all, He convicts us of our sins (John 16:8-11). It is the Holy Spirit, not our own consciences, that reveals to us what is truly right and wrong. He acts as that "buzz" in our spirit that warns us when we're heading for disaster. In this role, He also reveals truth to us. This is why Christians across the ages have prayed for wisdom when situations beyond them arise in their lives. They have the One who convicts and illuminates our very souls living right inside of them.

He is also the agent of change in our lives (Philippians 2:13, Acts 15:8-9). When you hear a sermon or go to a Bible study and feel that conviction that makes you want to change and somehow gives you the power to even do so at the same time, that is the Holy Spirit working in you. Truly, it is only through the Holy Spirit that we are even able to change. It's not the sermon itself or even the Bible

---

[110] Which stinks, because I was really hoping that was one of those Spiritual Gift things, so I wouldn't have to work so hard to figure out which train was going to get to Boston first.

study itself, but the Holy Spirit working in our lives that inspires and empowers us to make changes no matter how small or large.

Back in Jr. High, I met a guy—who I'll call "Bob"—who became a very dear friend to me. Bob, at the time I met him, was considered somewhat of a thug. He smoked, drank, stole, and lived to fulfill his own pleasures. Though I didn't become friends with Bob to convert him, the result of my own deepening walk with God caused me to try to convict him of his sins and attempt to get him to repent. My friend David Lake and I would tag team him and even "force" him to come to church with us. Bob, though he cared for our friendship, resented our attempts to convict him and pushed away from God. After years of trying our hand at being God's voice of conviction, we had nothing to show for our attempts.

One random night, while David[111] and I were helping at youth group, Bob (who claimed he would burst into flames if he stepped foot in a church) showed up with a smile on his face. Through no work David or I could have done, God's Spirit got ahold of Bob and convicted him of his need for a Savior and showed him the emptiness of the things he was trying to find his hope in. That night, Bob recounted to us how he "simply could not explain" what had happened, but that he had given his life to Christ.

In that moment, he stopped smoking, drinking, and doing drugs cold turkey. I've heard stories of that happening from other people, but never really believed they were true. I figured they were simply embellished stories to make the speaker sound better, but this was exactly the case with Bob. The Holy Spirit came into Bob and changed his life. Just a few years later, when we were still in our mid-twenties, I was blessed to sit at Bob's bedside as he fought a losing

---

[111] Fun fact: David once shaved his entire body for a swim meet. Not content with that alone, Dave wore a plunger to school the next day in order to psych himself up for the meet. That has nothing to do with anything; it's just awesome.

battle against a sudden outburst of an extremely rare and extremely aggressive cancer and take a final communion with him. God's Spirit, and God's Spirit alone, came alongside Bob and became the agent of change in his life. Praise God that He did. Just a few short days later, David and I, along with several other friends, stood together as Bob was lowered into his physical body's final resting place. Thanks to God's miraculous grace and indwelling power, we knew that though Bob's body was laid to rest, his spirit was merely "sleeping" and waiting for the Final Judgment.

In addition to conviction, illumination, and change, the Holy Spirit also brings us needed assurance. Romans 8:16 informs us that it is the Spirit that reminds us (or testifies) that we are children of God. This promise is also echoed back in 1 John 3:23-24. It is the Spirit that assures us we are in Christ and have been purchased by Him. We are a people filled with doubt, but it is God's Spirit that comes alongside of us to take that doubt and cast it away. We know that we belong to Christ because the Spirit of Christ lives in us.

Perhaps the most commonly stated aspect of God's work in our lives through His Spirit is that of a guide. Romans 8:9 assures us that as followers of Jesus Christ, we are no longer in our flesh, but in the Spirit. It also tells us that the Spirit in us is the Spirit of Christ Himself. The imagery used in many places in the Bible is that of flesh vs. spirit. It states that a life that follows the flesh (or mind set on the flesh) is death to us, but that true life is found in the guidance of the Holy Spirit. In this capacity, the Holy Spirit is our teacher of spiritual truths (John 14:26, John 16:13, 1 Corinthians 2:14).

What a teacher to have! How many books in your personal library do you have that the author of the book is available to you directly and personally at any time to answer any question and help you understand the meaning? Most certainly, the answer is one. God's Spirit is our guide and teacher of spiritual truths and, as the Author of the Bible, is available to us 24/7 if we just seek Him.

In addition to this, He is our mouthpiece in witnessing to others. Luke 12:11-12 says not to worry when we are brought before rulers and those in power because God's Spirit will give us what to say. This is a great promise because when we attempt to share Christ with others, we often don't know what to say. Our own words have no power to convince or convict at all; it is the Spirit of God Who gives us the words we're looking for.

His work doesn't stop there. Not only does the Holy Spirit go before us when it comes to men, He also is the one who intercedes for us in prayer. Romans 8:26-27 says that He goes before God in prayer on our behalf with groaning too deep for words as He searches our very hearts. He is our Advocate before the Father. Jesus said that He was going away, but that He would leave His Spirit to be our Comforter, and this is one of the ways He accomplishes that. He is our powerful Helper, and He gives us a power we don't deserve! As sinners, we deserve to be cast out into "weeping and gnashing of teeth," but through God's Spirit, we are granted a personal, fear-free audience with the King of the universe. Acts 1:8 affirms that we have power in prayer through Him. Take a moment and look it up in your own Bible.

Acts 15:8-9 also tells us that it is He who purifies our hearts. He is the One that cleanses us from the defilement of sin and shame. Truly, the "Helper" has many great roles in our lives. He is God within us. Through Him and Him alone are we to go through the process called sanctification (1 Thessalonians 4:1-8, 5:23-24). As we are dead branches that are grafted into Christ the Vine (John 15: 4-7), we are powerless without the Spirit. As A. W. Tozer has said:

> It is quite plain in the Scriptural revelation that spiritual things are hidden by a veil, and by nature, a human does not have the ability to comprehend and get hold of them. He comes up against a blank wall. He takes doctrine and texts and proofs and creeds and theology, and lays them up like a

wall—but he cannot find the gate! He stands in the darkness and all about him is intellectual knowledge of God—but not the knowledge of God, for there is a difference between the intellectual knowledge of God and the Spirit-revealed knowledge[112].

Unfortunately, this is the danger we run into in going through a course with so much good information about God. We may well only produce an intellectual knowledge of Him with no spiritual knowledge of Him. My prayer for both you and myself is that we seek and allow the Holy Spirit to be the One who drives us, not just to information, but also to transformation from deep within. Only He can do such a thing.

Before we move on to the next lesson, I want to ask you to take a personal power inventory. Dr. Vance Havner was once quoted as saying that if the Holy Spirit were to withdraw from today's church, on the average 90% of its activities would go unhindered. How much of your life is lived in your own power? How often do you struggle to take control by all means necessary? While it is striking and disheartening that Dr. Havner's words may be true for the average church, it is almost certain that his words ring true for the average Christian.

Ask yourself, "How much of what I'm trying to do for God is done in my own power?" Go ahead. Take a sheet of paper and think of 5-10 things that show that you're trying to do this under your own prowess. Perhaps you even began reading this book and going through this journey determined to make significant changes under your own power. It cannot be done. Even if it looks like you have made a success here and there, the changes will not long last if the Holy Spirit does not direct it.

---

[112] Tozer, A. W. *When He is Come,* Christian Publications, 1968.

As (post)modern men and women, we do all we can to keep from looking weak. We even go before God at times trying to earn His approval by being "strong and powerful in Him". You cannot be powerful in yourself and be powerful in God at the same time. That is an impossible contradiction. The truth is that we are only strong when we are weak in ourselves. 2 Corinthians 12:9-10 says, "He said to me, 'My grace is sufficient for you, for My power is made perfect in weakness. Therefore I will boast all the more gladly about my weakness, so that Christ's power may rest on me. That is why, for Christ's sake, I delight in weakness, in insults, in hardships, in persecutions, in difficulties. For when I am weak, then I am strong."

St. Augustine of Hippo, an early shaper of the Christian faith, summed this up by saying, "Let me not be my own life, for when I live of myself I lived evilly: I was death to myself. But in You I live again".[113] How much of our lives are lived in ourselves? How can we now turn our lives over, not simply to the salvation of Christ, but the sanctification of the Holy Spirit?

---

[113] Augustine of Hippo, *Confessions* XII: 10

Lesson 8 Assignment Sheet

1. Daily Quiet Time
   a. As you spend time with God this week, try to become more aware of how much you are trying to do the work and how much you're allowing "the Helper" to work in you. Refer to Philippians 1:6 and 2:13. Take some time to complete the spiritual inventory mentioned at the end of this lesson.

2. Scripture Memorization
   a. 2 Corinthians 5:17, 1 John 4:8, Revelation 4:8b, John 15:7-8, Psalm 119:11, Psalm 119:105, 1 John 5:11-12, John 16:24, and 1 Corinthians 10:13.
   b. Learn Proverbs 3:5-6.

3. Prayer partnership
   a. Invite the Holy Spirit into your prayer time.
   b. Ask each other how much of your weekly efforts towards God are done in your own power.

4. Quiet Time Log
   a. Submit your QTL to your disciple-maker for review.
   b. Start a new QTL.

> "Trust in the Lord with all your heart and do not lean on your own understanding. In all your ways acknowledge Him, and He will make your paths straight."
>
> Proverbs 3:5-6 (NASB)

Lesson 9—

Committing to Christ's Body

Back in 2009, I was a Senior Accounts Manager for Dell Computers. Working in the tech industry, you run into all sorts of characters. These ranged from the most savvy tech geeks[114] who lived and breathed the digital age like it was the purest form of oxygen imaginable, all the way down to the person who didn't know a thing about computers, but found themselves learning the ropes to make the "big bucks" promised right around the corner.

One of the many amazing people I met in my time in the corporate world was Johnny. Johnny was something of an enigma. Having been very successful as a salesman in the auto industry, Johnny was hired to work in his true area of passion in the computer world. Being very enigmatic, intelligent, and boisterously outspoken, Johnny did very well selling software and peripherals as a member of the sales support team.

When I met Johnny a few years back, I was immediately taken by how personable he was both with co-workers and on the phone with customers. If you needed a customer smoothed over a little, Johnny was the guy to go to. Yet, as I got to know him a little better, I found out that though he relished in personal interaction at work, his home life was dedicated to one thing: *World of Warcraft*. If you're unfamiliar, WoW was/is a Massive Multiplayer Online

---

[114] My kind of people.

Role-Playing Game (MMORPG). The purpose of the game is to create a fantasy character and then hone them through online battle into the best dwarf, mage, or elf you can. With all the time it takes to invest in this digital second life, many people start to have difficultly separating themselves from their character. They're like sports fanatics who wear the team colors at all times, check their smartphones for updates constantly, and even bring an in-ear radio with them to listen to news about their team 24/7. Except with elves, rather than sports stars.

Some people, like my old friend Johnny, if they're not careful, can literally lose themselves in this creation of theirs and spend every waking moment treating the "real" world as a chore they have to get through to support their "second life" addiction. "Places" like WoW have become such a beacon for people to lose themselves in that a real psychologist opened up a "real" practice within the WoW game space and began seeing patients at one point. In our day and age it is entirely possible to treat reality as if it were the dream we awake from the second our digital self is booted up.

This has fundamentally changed certain aspects of society for millions of people. In reality, WoW is just one of many MMORPGs, and MMORPGs are a small category in the plethora of options we have to "live" a life that's not truly ours at all. It's easier than ever to get the feeling of community and interaction with other human beings without ever truly interacting with human beings on a real level. The most visited website in the world today, after all, is Facebook. Now, don't get me wrong, I love Facebook and all the many ways that it truly can connect you with people you haven't seen since high school[115] (and possibly never wanted to). For all their

---

[115] When I was a kid, the *Back to the Future* movies told me we'd have flying cars by 2015. Instead, we got the unprecedented dominance of social media and the return of the dreaded Furby. I'm still waiting for my pink hoverboard!

worth, however, social media sites are not a true form of personal one-on-one interaction.

These "second lives" we live in digital space often become a replacement for the true and honest community that we were created for. This problem becomes even larger when we consider the role of the Church. Many cutting-edge churches now offer options where you can stay at home and still be a part of the "community." Instead of going to church, you can now connect with them on their social sites. After all, why should you have to inconvenience yourself with things like traffic and annoying people to meet with God when God is all around and open to us at any time?

As a society, we have begun to lose the meaning of authentic community. Chuck Colson, in his work entitled *The Body*, said of this:

> Many Christians are infected with the most virulent virus of modern American life, what sociologist Robert Bellah calls 'radical individualism.' They concentrate on personal obedience to Christ as if all that matters is 'Jesus and me,' but in so doing miss the point altogether…Christianity is not a solitary belief system. Any genuine resurgence of Christianity, as history demonstrates, depends on a reawakening and renewal of that which is the essence of the faith—that is, the people of God, the new society, the Body of Christ, which is made manifest to the world—the Church. There is no such thing as Christianity apart from the Church[116].

React to that last statement. Can you have authentic Church contained within a purely online experience? Could you witness to someone through the digital halls of WoW and thereby create a

---

[116] Colson, Chuck. *The Body*, W Publishing Group: Nashville, TN, 1992, 32.

church? Perhaps. I suppose anything is possible in today's world. But, that's not what we're called to as our primary outlet. In this lesson, we will examine the importance of community and commitment to a local body of believers. It is important, then, that you first understand what the Church is. That is, you need to understand what many Christians call the "Big-C" Church.

The church (with a little c) is a building that we often pass by on our way to work and possibly even consider going into once or twice a year. The Church (with a big C) is the Body of Christ comprised of all persons who have given their life to the Son of God and are receiving their life from Him. If you're a Christian, you're a part of the "Big-C" Church automatically whether you attend a "small-c" church or not. The problem is, however, that many people have gotten into a pattern of thinking that you can have one without the other. You cannot.

I want you to clearly hear what I'm saying on this, so I'm going to point out what I am definitely *not* saying, first. I'm not saying that you absolutely must meet in a brick and mortar building that holds specific services at specific times. For many, however, this will be the best choice. Church happens when God's people get together in His Name in many settings. House churches and missions are just a couple other examples of Church without the church. The problems begin when you start thinking that you absolutely don't need the little-c church at all to be the Big-C Church. Meeting with a local congregation of believers was always a part of God's plan for the life of every follower of Jesus Christ.

Take, for example, the Church that sprung up in the Book of Acts. This is often referred to as the "perfect" model for what "Church" should look like. In this period of Biblical history, the disciples got together with everyone they could who was beginning to believe in Jesus Christ and "did life together." We find that they shared everything and met often. In fact, they seemed to meet daily…at minimum[117]. They were no longer caught up with going to church, but becoming the Church. It wasn't about attending ABC Community Church, it was about living as the Church every day, in every way, to every place, to every person.

Being the "ideal" model, it doesn't take long for these disciples (and later Paul) to go out and begin to start churches in other cities. Something remarkable in all of this was that whether or not what was planted ended up looking like the Acts 2 church of communal living (which did not make it for various reasons), or something like the synagogue system that was common to their day, persons who followed Christ were encouraged strongly not to give up meeting together. There was a sense of community, of one-on-one interaction that prevailed as the *dominant* mode of living out life as a disciple.

To put it plainly, the disciples, and all that followed after them, made it a habit to not only be the Church, but to meet together as a church. This is why, for all of its imperfections, even Church-leadership experts like Bill Hybels are still proclaiming boldly to this day that "the local church is the hope of the world[118]." Can you be the Church and not attend church? Not long-term. There is a fellowship element that is implicit in a life of discipleship. Whether we like it or not, we can't fully trade Internet church services for meeting with fellow brothers-and-sisters-in-Christ on a regular basis (though you can catch the service online during bouts of sickness with my full blessing).

If it is true that we must meet together as the Church regularly as a part of our discipleship journey, then we need to answer the question, "What should my commitment to the Church/church be?" To answer this, we'll look at six key elements or areas. What

---

[117] Imagine going to church every day. If that springs fear into your heart, you probably need to take a deep look at what real Church should be.

[118] Hybels, Bill. *Courageous Leadership,* Zondervan: Grand Rapids, MI, 2008, 7.

follows may or may not be the sum of what it takes to have a church and be the Church, but you cannot claim either and not at least include these. Some of these elements are no-brainers. Others may need some explanation. One or more of them may scare you or challenge you a little, but all are Biblical elements that explain what our commitment to a local Body of believers must be as disciples of the living Christ.

The first area we must look at is attendance. As we have already elaborated upon above, church attendance is rarely seen as a "must" these days. In years past—I'm told by those further along in life than myself—it was not only common to attend church every week, but expected. Many a young man (myself included here and there) was dragged unwillingly to church and made to sit there and not make a sound because that was simply what good Christian people did. We are no longer in that mythical Christian society.

Statistically, if you were born in the late-nineties or later, you were probably not "forced" to go to church by your parents. If you did go to church, you were likely C.E.O. Christians[119]. If your family was "really spiritual," you may have attended church once or twice when it wasn't a Christmas or Easter. service. Once you reached an age where you could decide for yourself, you likely didn't go to church simply because it was such a habit not to. Besides, churches, as we all know, are simply filled with hypocrites[120]. Going to church on a weekly basis, for some, would just seem strange.

---

[119] C.E.O. stands for "Christmas and Easter Only". One Easter a few years ago, Lifechurch.tv pastor Craig Groeschel was bold enough to ask the audience what they got for Christmas. When they looked confused, he reminded them sweetly that that was the last time he had seen many of them. To which I went, "Ooohhhh, pastor burn."

[120] It's hard to use that argument when people own up to their junk. I'm a hypocrite at times. It happens. I try not to be. But we, as people, have this tendency to fall short. Theologically, this is called our "sin nature."

No matter how committed to our church we are, we get an image of the person who does attend regularly as that elderly lady who is quite literally there every second the doors are open. If it's not Granny Goodness, then it's that religious nut who, like the Pharisees, comes regularly just to prove to God that they've got what it takes to make it to heaven. It just seems strange in our Facebook society to ask people to make attendance at Church/church a habit, right? I mean, what sort of people would that make us?

No matter how strange we think it is, as disciples of Jesus Christ, we are following the example of a Man who made worship attendance a habit. That's right, Jesus attended synagogues regularly. Luke 4:16 tells us that it was Jesus' custom to attend what we now call church service and meet with the Church. Isn't that strange? If anyone in the history of the world had an excuse to skip church service, certainly it was Jesus! Can you imagine that pastoral call?

"Hello, yes may I speak to Jesus Christ, please?"

"I Am He."

"Oh, good. Well, Jesus, this is Pastor John Smith over at ABC Community Church. I'll cut right to the point. Your attendance is strikingly low, and although you regularly tithe, I wanted to see what possible reason You could have for not being at church."

"Well, Pastor Smith. I AM. I'm God. I sort of wrote the book you're going to be preaching from this Sunday. I know it so much better than you do, and I just figured I could benefit from sleeping in. There's just so much to do as God, you know?"

Think about it. Jesus is God. Can you imagine what He must have been thinking when attending synagogue and hearing people read the Words that He penned through the ages and trying to teach Him from it? It almost sounds ludicrous to really think about it. And yet, Jesus' custom was to attend church. In fact, it has also been the custom of all disciples throughout time who follow after Him. The synagogue system Jesus attended was simply replaced with the beautiful bride we now call the Church.

Hebrews 10:24-25 is another great place to look to see what the Bible itself has to say about this topic. In this verse, we see that our attendance in worship is an encouragement to other believers. The writer of Hebrews asks us not to give up assembling together "as is the habit of some." Truly, one aspect of our discipleship is to meet as the Church in the church. What this looks like may change with culture to some degree, but the core of it will not.

I am not here endorsing one specific denomination. I will not urge you toward one church rather than its brother across the street. Where you meet is largely up to you and God in you. What I will say, however, is that as a disciple it is time to stop dating the church. Stop "church shopping." Don't go on pretending that you're ever going to find the "perfect church." The problem with all churches everywhere is that they're filled with people just like us. We will never find a "perfect church," and yet we use that as an excuse to avoid the deep level of community and commitment that Jesus is calling us to[121].

In the end, the only thing you need to know is if this church clings to Christ and teaches truth. Everything else, to some degree or another, is simply a personal wish list similar to what many people make (consciously or not) when they are looking for a dating partner. If you find a church near you that honestly teaches truth and you feel God calling you to it, the rest is simply a matter of your preferences. I'll admit that the way God has wired you to interact with Him can certainly play a role in which particular church you end up committing to, just like the true function of dating, but you must eventually commit.

---

[121] I firmly believe that God calls people to certain churches, just as He calls the pastor to the church. If God isn't releasing you from a church, it's time to stop complaining about its perceived inadequacies and start doing the hard work of giving your life to the Body. Perhaps that church is just waiting for you to start working on that issue you're sore over.

If you're the type that's prone to divorce your church (for that is really what you're doing) over one of your preferences not being met, it's time to grow up. You're not acting like a disciple in that case. You're being a consumer and caring only for what that church is doing for you. God is calling us to a mature relationship with a specific cell in His Body. Mature relationships never involve one party leaving because their feelings got hurt once or the other person's musical tastes is just a little different[122].

Of course, there does exist a number of valid reasons as to why you may leave one church for another one. Perhaps you're relocating to another city, for example. Perhaps the church follows after a heresy that cannot be uprooted. These are some of the few valid reasons that exist to leave one church for another. In any case, you must get to a point where you are mature enough in your relationship with a local body that you won't jump ship if they change the color of the paint on the walls[123].

Here you may say, "But my church doesn't have enough emphasis on missions and I want to be a part of a Missional Body," or something of the like. You certainly could divorce your church over a reason like this...or you could start being more missional yourself and invite others in that cell of Christ's Body to do the same. As disciples, we're all called to do the work of ministry. It's not simply the job of those who are "paid" to do it. Your pastor serves an indispensible role, which we'll get to in a moment, but one of their biggest roles is to mobilize *you* to take on the work of ministry, not to do it all for you. If you see a need in your church that you're considering leaving them over, talk to the pastoral staff and volunteer

---

[122] Ooooh, pastor burn.

[123] Or, gasp, change music styles! Charles Spurgeon reportedly called his church's music ministry department "the war room" because so many people got up in arms over their musical preferences being stepped on with each change the team would make.

to create that program yourself. If you seriously feel that you could not do this, at least work to find someone who will. Maybe this "sore spot" is on someone else's heart, but they're just waiting for someone else to speak up and get moving on it. This is how the church acts like the Church and not simply consumers who scream, "feed me," and leave in a huff if no one listens to their whining cries[124].

The second area we need to examine is our giving and tithing. Believe me, I have been at a number of churches in the past that approached this topic absolutely wrong and have turned me away from the "desire" to give money to them. I've been in churches where it feels like the pastor is holding a gun to your head and telling you that if you don't put money in the bucket, then you're going to hell. Ironically, that same pastor is the one driving an expensive car and living in an expensive house that is out of sync with where he is called to and how much he is giving to the poor. I've been to those churches before. I've even seen them on TV.

The cold hard fact, however, is that tithing is a part of our discipleship commitment. Let me say that again. Your use of "your" money is an aspect of your discipleship just as much as anything else. In fact, it is often the single hardest aspect for people to give over to God. We have no problem agreeing with lessons about our misunderstanding of God and finding that He is a God who has our best interests at heart, but if a preacher starts talking about your checkbook, you're ready to divorce that church and leave that second[125].

Truly, many churches have tackled this financial aspect of our discipleship journey very wrongly. That doesn't mean, however, that

---

[124] I hope you don't think I'm being a jerk here. As I said, I'm a very honest person and this is something that just needed to be said straightforward and honestly. Or, maybe I'm just a jerk.

[125] And the church doesn't even get half of your money in the divorce. Bah dum tss.

we're excused from it. In fact, I would say the very reason we really and truly, deep down, despise it when people start telling us "God wants our money" is that money is truly our god. If money itself isn't, the stuff it buys us may very well be. Let's take a look for a moment at the life of the "rich young ruler."

The story of the "rich young ruler" is a favorite for pastors. In it, a young man comes to Jesus and asks him what he must do to inherit eternal life. Notice right away the language used. "Inherit" is a term typically used when talking about someone dying and leaving behind stuff and money, is it not? Now, I don't know about you, but as a pastor, this is a dream question. This guy comes up to Jesus and is ready to "get saved." So what does Jesus do? He tells him that "God loves him and has a wonderful plan for his life," right? Wrong. Jesus does something that evangelism experts would likely never tell you to do to someone who is eager to meet Christ. He forces this man to evaluate his life. He calls out this man's true god.

Read through Luke 18:18-30 in your own Bible. Read it two or three times. No, really, read it. What do you notice? Jesus doesn't play around with this guy. We don't see Jesus thanking the guy for his enthusiasm at all. Instead, Jesus very quickly identifies the real gods that this man is following after, which are his possessions and wealth. Jesus calls out this other god and tells the young man that he must divorce that god before he can be a part of Jesus' redeemed bride. In all honesty, we're more often the rich young ruler than we are the disciples that speak up in the next couple of verses.

Today's world has taught us since we were just out of the womb to acquire stuff and hoard as much money as we can. The problem is that Jesus tells us we are to give up everything and follow Him. In fact, just two chapters earlier in Luke 16:13 we see the heart of why this is a discipleship issue. You cannot serve God and wealth. They are both masters, and you cannot have two.

The reason why tithing is important to your discipleship is that it is a visible, tangible way you show God and yourself that wealth is not your master and you trust God to provide for you. That's it. As followers of Jesus, we are called to give a tithe (typically 10% of our earnings) *first*—before we pay any bills or put food in our children's mouths. We give from our "first fruits" as a symbol of the fact that we are not mastered by our money and possessions, knowing that God will provide for us (and our hungry children). If we "can't" do this, then money actually possesses us, and God is not truly our God. Giving of the "first fruits" of what we earn is a small way to help make sure that God is seated on the throne of our hearts and not shiny things. There is no true Health-and-Wealth Gospel when it comes to material possessions and earthly wealth; Christ calls us to give that junk up, not hoard as much as we can[126].

This is also the only way the little-c church can survive. Pastors, ministries, the missions we pray for where people in China will come to know God, even that small group that prompted you to read this book, all of them are funded by your tithe. And the shocking thing is, God designed it this way, not your pastor. God chose to provide for the little-c church and grow the Big-C church by having the Big-C Church plow the way. Take it up with Jesus if you like, but the fact of the matter is that if Christians would just take this aspect of their discipleship seriously and tithe as God requires, the church and the Church would be able to do what it does best. It would be able to help people out in the community that have fallen behind on their bills, it would be able to open a food pantry for the poor, it would be able to send people on missions. It may even be able to pay your pastor well enough that he doesn't have to work two or three jobs.

The average church has just near 20-30% of its people at most funding 90% of the ministry that happens. Just think of what could happen if 90% of the people were on board!!! That is a discipleship

---

[126] Which is why you should send all of your money to my address, which is... nah, just kidding. That would be super shady, right? But seriously, the solid-gold plating on my swimming pool is wearing off, so where's that check?

issue, not an invasive cry for you to open up your pocket book. Again, this is between you and Jesus, not you and your pastor. I think you'll find that Jesus makes much stronger demands. Whereas your pastor will likely harangue you for a measly 10%, Jesus asks and requires that we give Him everything and hold nothing back.

It may also help you to know that it isn't really yours anyway. Sure you "earned" it by working for it...but it isn't yours. Scripture says the earth and everything in it belongs to God. What you have, you've been given by Him as a steward. You're watching out for God's money and God's things. If God asked you to give them up, He would have the right to. Truly, He often does this in our discipleship process for our own good, because He has our best interests at heart and cannot stand to see us in bondage to a false master. So, the next time you look at your stuff and your checkbook, recognize that it is God's and that you literally own none of it. You are, as you should remember, nothing but dust (Psalm 103).

When you think you own stuff and get caught up in the process of owning as much of it as you can, in reality the stuff turns around and begins to own you and usurps God's place in our hearts. Jesus says your heart is where your treasure lies. What you treasure, there your heart will be also. Do you treasure God or stuff[127]? It's a hard question, but one that must be asked. If you couldn't give up _____ if God asked you to, then _____ is your treasure and is likely in God's spot in your heart. You don't own anything. Even your body, as 1 Corinthians 6:19-20 tells us, has been bought with a price and is His.

I could go on and on with this topic simply because it is the single most misunderstood and wrongly accused topic in the whole of our Christian walk. But, I will stop here. Study verses like 2 Corinthians

---

[127] I'll admit it, this one is hard for me. I like shiny things. New technology seems to come out every day. I mean, come on, I have to have an iEverything to function, right? Gotta satiate my iGottahaveits.

9:7, Hebrews 13:16, and Malachi 3:10, if you're interested in looking further into this topic. I also urge you with all that's in me to immediately go through *Financial Peace University* by Dave Ramsey the very second it is offered in your area. If it's not offered in your area, pick up *The Total Money Makeover* and start working through that book. You must begin to learn what God calls us to do with His stuff if you are to be a good steward.

The next area in your commitment to your local church is that of your pastor. Hebrews 13:17 says that God has given us pastors as those put in place to watch over our souls[128]. Our response should be respect, support, and encouragement. Quite literally, this verse tells us that we should obey and submit to them. That, of course, sounds very negative in today's "me-centered" culture. It shouldn't be.

There's a lot that is assumed in the context of this verse. Most prominently, the assumption is that your pastor is properly submitting to and obeying Christ first. I've seen both sides. I have been blessed with wonderful senior pastors who are submitting to Christ and I have seen, very close to home, pastors who don't follow God's will and the destruction they can cause. The simple fact is, however, it takes a healthy pastor to have a healthy church. If your pastor is not spiritually, mentally, and emotionally (to some degree even physically healthy) the church cannot have a deep and abiding health in itself.

I've spent the better part of two decades of my life in retail sales. As a part of that, I took the wildest ride I could have ever imagined entering the corporate world during the lowest point in the economic recession. I have come into work and been told that my department no longer exists and been one of only a handful to move on to another role that may or may not exist for much longer. I've moved departments, changed managers, frequently moved desks, and saw

---

[128] Not "to be the only one allowed to do ministry since, after all we're paying them to do it."

many people have to leave in the name of corporate restructuring. At the same time, I was responsible to earn the company millions of dollars each quarter in order to keep my job. Believe me, I've seen some crazy stuff in the work world, but nothing I've personally done compares to the weight of the responsibility of being a pastor. Nor does the reward. God gives us pastors (literally shepherds) to watch over our souls. Our response to a good pastor (as God would define them, not our own personal definition) should be respect, support, and trust.

As one who gave up a corporate career to devote his life to the ministry, I've seen church members do and say horrible things to their pastor that far exceed even my days in "corporate restructuring." I've known way too many shepherds whose flock have abused, taken advantage of, and worked to subtly (and not so subtly) tear them down. As a pastor, you rarely hear the words "thank you" spoken. And yet, you're expected to put countless hours into sermon prep, another set of countless hours making hospital visits, attending (and leading) events, and being ready at all hours of the night to deal with any and all personal concerns. You're expected to put your family on hold at a moment's notice, raise and entertain other people's children, and all the while keep the church "running" as if it were a local business. Then, if someone takes one word wrong, or God starts stepping on their toes through a sermon, you're suddenly the worst thing that ever happened to that place. While this certainly isn't the day-to-day norm, of course, it is certainly all too common.

Please don't get me wrong, all of those duties come with being a pastor, and they should be done joyfully. I can say without hesitation that accepting a calling into vocational ministry is a blessing and a treasure. But, we as followers of Christ are called to love one another. We're called to bear one another's burdens. We're told not to gossip, not to slander. We're told to take care of those in need. We're even told that there is a proper process for airing grievances with one another. What we forget is that this list applies to our attitude and relationship with our pastor, too. In fact, 1 Timothy 5:17 says that they should receive double honor.

When was the last time you honestly thanked your pastor? Today sounds like a good day for that. Forgive me for this little tirade, but in the name of decency and etiquette your pastor either can't or won't say these things to your church. Maybe it's time for your church to take "Pastor's appreciation month[129]" seriously. Maybe that month shouldn't be the only month the church goes out of their way to make the pastor (and their family, who make even greater sacrifices to allow the pastor to do all of these things) feel appreciated. If this sounds a little harsh, I apologize. Perhaps you've supported your pastor in amazing and visible ways before your congregation. What if you're in the minority, though? Just imagine the spiritual growth and health your church can experience if the church itself is supporting its shepherd rather than giving him "death by sheep bites."

Remember, your pastor has a certain well-defined list of qualities he must continue to exude, as I mentioned above. There is certainly a process for dealing with pastors who are not taking their role as shepherd and leader seriously. That process should not, however, include any of the following: undermining, gossip, public campaigns, private meetings, power plays, political maneuvering, or even just a cold shoulder. The deep truth in this is that if your pastor becomes unhealthy it is difficult for the church to be healthy. Healthy churches grow and honor God. Unhealthy churches, on the other hand, shrivel and become inward-focused to the grave. If you are passionate about seeing the Church and your church grow, one of your spiritual duties is to fight for your pastor. After all, God has entrusted headship over your congregation to this person. He goes before God so that he can shepherd and lead as God has asked him to as he goes before the people.

---

[129] October, just in case you were wondering.

What would happen in your congregation if even a vocal minority started publically and privately honoring, uplifting, and taking care of your pastor? How would that free him up to seek God more passionately and, thereby, serve your congregation with even more power, energy, zest, positivity, and spiritual health? I promise, following this advice will pay back in spades. Healthy pastors are essential to fostering healthy churches, and just as your pastor has a role from God to shepherd and lead your congregation; your congregation must honor, respect, trust, and uplift your pastor. I promise a healthier Church if you do[130].

A fourth commitment we must make as disciples of Christ is to fellow believers. Biblically, we are commanded to bear one another's burdens and to encourage each other toward love and good deeds. We are responsible for the one another's growth. Proverbs 27:17 tells us that just as "iron sharpens iron, so one man sharpens another." Galatians 6:2 tells us that we are to "bear one another's burdens, and thereby fulfill the law of Christ." John 13:35 (my youth pastor growing up, Joe Ganahl's favorite verse) says that, "This is how they will know that you are My [Jesus'] disciples, by your love for one another."

No Christian man or woman is an island. We cannot live in isolation. We were created for community. As such, we have a responsibility for each other in our discipleship. No matter if you're extroverted or introverted, you are called to be a part of the lives of others. Literally, we all make up the Body of Christ. We all have our unique differences, but those differences are given to us so that Christ's Body may be fully functional. In our own bodies, the

---

[130] I imagine someone may assume I'm passive-aggressively writing from experience at my own church. Luckily, God has blessed me with a supportive congregation. However, I have watched too many close friends and fellow pastors work through the pains described above. Some have even left the ministry to, get this, provide a healthier environment for their family.

hand serves a different function than the eye. They look different, move different, and do very different things, but you could not fully function without these two unique parts working together in harmony. Likewise, Jesus' Body, of which we are but a cell, cannot function without harmony in diversity.

We're called to lift each other up. We're called to encourage one another, train one another, share life with one another. We have a role to play in the Body of Christ. We have a unique function the rest of the Body cannot do without. Through it all, we're called to love one another. Jesus even said that this very thing would be the one and only way that "they" (the rest of the world) would recognize us as His disciples. If we are disciples of Christ, we love each other as He loved and work the task that He gave us to work.

This brings us to the fifth area of commitment, which is service or ministry. Everyone within the Body of believers has a responsibility to find and do what God called him/her to do in the life of the Church. Look at the early church's response to the diversity of needs they came across as recorded in Acts 6:1-3. Take a stroll through Romans 12:1-4 and see this very message echoed back. The Bible makes it clear that we all have a role to play as a part of His Body, that that role is unique to how He has gifted us, and if we don't engage in that role, the Body suffers.

The last area of commitment in the context of a local Body/ church we are commanded to make is that of growth. Matthew 28:19-20, Acts 2:41-47, Acts 5:14, Hebrews 5:12-14, and 2 Peter 3:18 (among others) make it clear that we have a responsibility for spiritual growth in at least two areas. First, you are responsible for your personal spiritual growth. Notice, I did not say that your pastor or small group leader, parent or spouse, was responsible for this. Remember, your pastor is responsible to keep guard over your soul as a shepherd watches his sheep to keep the wolves away and to deliver the Word of God. Your pastor is not responsible for your personal spiritual growth. That task is yours. Certainly, your pastor is and should be a catalyst that is indispensible to that process, but, ultimately, the responsibility falls on you.

The second aspect of this is that you are also responsible for the growth of your church and the Church. Every single believer is called to follow the words of Jesus (remember they were His last) to go and make disciples. Your pastor should certainly be at the forefront of this, but it is your job to grow your church and the Church. It is your job to become discipled (which you are beginning here and must continue throughout your life) and to then disciple others. If you are a believer in Jesus Christ, you are a minister of His Gospel. There is no Plan B.

On a sheet of paper, after you have read the five sets of verses I mentioned two paragraphs above from your own Bible, write out five practical ways you can deepen your commitment to your church and the Church. Talk this over with your discipleship group, as well as your disciple-maker this week. In closing up this lesson, I want to bring to you this quote from Charles Spurgeon. Think about the implication that satan takes Christian fellowship more seriously than we, as Christians, often do. "Satan always hates Christian fellowship. It is his policy to keep Christians apart. He delights in anything that can divide saints from one another. He attaches far more importance to godly relationships than we do.[131]"

---

[131] Spurgeon, Charles. *Power over Satan*. Whitaker House: New Kensington, 2000, 81.

Lesson 9 Assignment Sheet

1. Daily Quiet Time
    a. Daily prayer, reading, and application of God's Word.
    b. As you spend time with God this week, spend some time evaluating your commitment level to the church where God has placed you. Review each of the areas in which we are to become committed (attendance, giving, your pastor, fellow believers, service or ministry, and growth) and write out five ways you can deepen your commitment to Christ through His Church.

2. Scripture Memorization
    a. Review 2 Corinthians 5:17, 1 John 4:8, Revelation 4:8b, John 15:7-8, Psalm 119:11, Psalm 119:105, 1 John 5:11-12, John 16:24, 1 Corinthians 10:13, and Proverbs 3:5-6.
    b. Learn John 15:4-5.

3. Find and complete at least 3 spiritual gifts inventories online prior to reading the next lesson
    a. Though they vary in quality, if you Google "Spiritual Gifts Inventory," you'll get several thousand hits. Take a few of the more reputable looking ones and compare the results.

4. Prayer Partnership
    a. Be sure you're talking to each other and praying a couple times in the week.

5. Quiet Time Log
   a. Turn your current QTL in to your disciple-maker.
   b. Begin a new QTL.

"Abide in Me, and I in you. As the branch cannot bear fruit of itself unless it abides in the vine, so neither can you unless you abide in Me. I am the vine, you are the branches; he who abides in Me and I in him, he bears much fruit, for apart from Me you can do nothing."

John 15:4-5 (NASB)

Lesson 10—

My Role in the Kingdom

I've already revealed to you that when I was younger I dreamt of becoming the next Hulk Hogan. A part of this desire stemmed from the fact that I was confident enough in myself to know that I could succeed in that industry if I gave my full heart to it[132]. When it comes to people I looked up to that I know I could not be, however, I would undoubtedly say Dick Van Dyke. If you've ever watched an episode of what is one of TV's all-time classic shows[133], you don't need to be told how talented Mr. Van Dyke is. Dick Van Dyke, the leading man on the show that bore his name, was and still is an amazingly talented human being.

It wouldn't take watching more than an episode or two of *The Dick Van Dyke Show* to see how talented an actor, a singer, a dancer, and a comedian, Dick is. Often times, he would be doing all of these simultaneously. On top of that, he was an astoundingly physical performer. Actors like Jim Carrey are still imitating Dick's style of physical comedy today. Dick was able to add an indescribable depth to each performance. It seems to me that Dick Van Dyke was given more than his share of talent, and I stand in awe of him for it.

---

[132] Though not so much anymore, since I've got dad gut going on.

[133] *The Dick Van Dyke Show* still holds up after all these years as one of the funniest TV experiences ever.

When you were born into this world, as a token of love for you, friends and family gave you gifts to celebrate the occasion. In much the same way, when you were "born again," the Spirit of God gave you certain gifts, as well. It is possible, according to which gifts you were given, to determine our place in the ministry of the Church. Just as Dick Van Dyke was born with something of a natural skill in acting, physical comedy, singing, and dancing that he developed throughout his life, when you came to receive new life from Christ, the Holy Spirit blessed you with certain skills He intends for you to develop and use to build His kingdom and glorify Him. James 1:16-17 says, "Do not be deceived, my beloved brethren. Every good thing given and every perfect gift is from above, coming down from the Father of lights, with whom there is no variation or shifting shadow."

According to James 1:16-17, God only gives His children good gifts. This makes perfect sense. If we have come to know God as a God of holy love Who has our best interests at heart, it follows that He gives His children only good gifts. Though what we see as good and what God sees as good may be slightly different, God has given you good gifts to use to glorify Him. These are what many call "spiritual gifts."

What are spiritual gifts? Dr. Charles Lake defines them as "supernatural or special abilities given by God to Christians for ministry [service] to others." The word "supernatural" stands out in this definition. Another childhood hero of mine was Superman. When I hear "supernatural abilities," my mind immediately goes to those "powers and abilities far beyond those of mortal men" that Superman possesses. I picture myself leaping tall buildings in single bounds and running faster than a speeding bullet. But that is not what Dr. Lake is talking about here[134].

---

[134] Too bad, too. Though I'm not sure how I'd look in tights, I'd be willing to make that sacrifice in order to get to fly and be invincible. Then people would be all like, "Look, up in the sky. It's that dude with serious dad gut."

Spiritual gifts may not be as bold as an invulnerable hide, but they are some great tools that can lead you to where your passion in God is met and show you a roadmap to where you would be happiest in life to serve. If you are keeping up with your weekly assignments, then you saw a bullet point to go online and take a couple spiritual gifts tests/inventories. If you haven't done this, please do so before this lesson is over. I just tabbed over to Google one second ago and typed in "Spiritual gifts test" and received back over 699,000 results, so this will not be a difficult task to find and complete an inventory.

Now, obviously, there are many different online tests you can find and they vary from very good to absolute garbage. If your church has the resource, it may be better for you to ask them for a paper copy of a spiritual gifts test they endorse. If you do not have this option at your church, then the online ones will suffice for now. The reason I ask you to take a couple (or several) online tests is simply because of the variance in them. Some will list certain spiritual gifts that others will not, such as the gift of celibacy[135]. In taking several inventories, you should see a pattern or a harmony develop. This will help reassure you that you're on the right path to finding what gifts are given to you.

Unfortunately, the fatal flaw of these tests is that they rest solely on how you see yourself. Therefore, it is imperative that you be painfully honest. If you fear public speaking, you probably shouldn't say that this skill is high on your natural abilities. You need to be honest on these inventories or risk pursuing something that you are not gifted in. When you go after gifts that you truly don't have, you

---

[135] When we took these inventories in college, my friend Rob came up with the gift of celibacy. Because of this (and his proud Norwegian heritage), we took to calling him Rob the Celibate Viking for a short time. Now he's just Rob, though. Just in case you tried to look him up in a phone book or something.

end up stealing glory away from God and depressing yourself, rather than finding the boundless joy of using what God has given you to magnify Him. This is a fancy way of saying that you don't get to pick your spiritual gifts. God gave them to you. You are supposed to discover them, but you don't get to be upset at God for gifting you with encouraging others rather than prophesy. If you have been "born again," you have at least one spiritual gift.

To illustrate this, my friend, "Rob the Celibate Viking," claimed for many years that he had the spiritual gift of celibacy; however, in reality, celibacy was pretty low on his list. I know, because I peeked. This leads me to point out that you need to be honest with what you find in your results. You're not picking a superpower; you're discovering how God has uniquely gifted you. If you find that mercy is high on your list, don't pretend that it's lower simply because you would rather have teaching as your top gift. It all comes down to honesty before God.

Before we discuss a few of the spiritual gifts found in Scripture, I need to point out that your gifts are in flux at times. When you're younger in Christ, you may find that one spiritual gift is your primary gift[136], only to find that it gives way to another when your situation changes. Though many times your spiritual gifts stay constant throughout your life, there are certainly times when God changes things up based on His needs for our situations. Someone who has little desire to lead people (such as Moses) may find God putting them into situations where leadership is needed. The wonderful truth, however, is that God qualifies the called, not the other way around[137].

Aside from the magic of the "interwebs," how else are your Spiritual Gifts discovered? First of all, our gifts are revealed to us

---

[136] Most inventories will point out your top three.

[137] That is an encouraging promise. God doesn't call us because we're qualified; He calls us and then makes us able to do what He has asked of us.

through prayer and study. If we are in communion with God, He will reassure us through His Word. This is the primary way that you should test the results of your spiritual gifts inventories. Another way of testing them would be to take your answers to a trusted friend who knows you well. This must be someone who knows your life well enough to both be honest with you and assess your findings through their own knowledge of God's working in your life. If you have several trusted confidants in your life, you may be able to take this to several friends and see what they find. God will often put people around us to help refine us into what He needs us to be. Remember, we are created for community and are called to sharpen one another.

The next step is that of exercise. If you feel that you have a spiritual gift, which is a gift God gave us to use and bless others, then beginning to use it is a natural way to see if that is really where your blessing lies. You'll both know and grow in your area of giftedness if you use it. If you feel that you really and truly have the gift of service, then you need to get out there and serve. If you're a leader, you need to read up on leadership and start leading.

Another place that will be helpful in assessing your spiritual gifts and the results of your spiritual gifts test is that of Body recognition. Does the part of the Body of Christ with which you are sharing your life recognize you to be gifted in this area or areas? For example, if you have felt that God is leading you to be a teacher, ask someone in a class or group you've taught whether they feel you have the gift of teaching. Just be sure that the person you ask is honest and loving (Ephesians 4:15). If everyone slept through the class you taught, you may need to re-evaluate and ask yourself if it was due to a lack of gifting in that area or just a novice level of skill that can be honed.

Two final ways to test your spiritual gifting are to look for fruitfulness/blessing and contentment. For this, look at John 15:8 from your own Bible. When you're doing what God has called you and gifted you to do, you will be fruitful and the Kingdom of God will be blessed. That may be the simplest acid test of all. There will also come with the use of your gifts a great contentment. There is absolutely nothing more fulfilling that finding and doing what God has made you for! This is the feeling people get that causes them to say, "I was born for this."

If you feel "led" to certain gifts automatically, should you seek these specific gifts? For this, I encourage you to read 1 Corinthians 12:1-11 and Romans 12:3-8 from your own Bible. Please be sure to do this now. These sections of Scripture let us know that gifts are received, not sought, from God only as He sees fit. They are discovered as they are exercised. Those who say they would love to know the will of God for their lives can find it to a large degree in how God has gifted them and in what areas He has placed their passions.

Since we have been alluding to the Spiritual Gifts for much of this lesson, I would like to briefly outline just a few of these as they are found in Scripture. This is not an extensive list, as various denominations may argue that one or another here and there should be on the list. This should, however, serve as a fairly solid list of what most all Christians agree are true spiritual gifts. As this is an introduction to discipleship, I will not give a detailed outline of each one. For that, I encourage you to check out other works that deal more specifically with this area.

Prophecy—The ability to proclaim the Word of God with authority and declare its truth in a clear, vital, and compelling way. The main purpose of prophecy is "for strengthening, encouraging, and comforting" (1 Corinthians 14:3). Examples may include: Preachers, elders, church leaders (2 Peter 1:19). One great work to look into for this gift would be Walter Bruggeman's *The Prophetic Imagination*, which outlines that prophecy is less about future telling or foretelling, but about forthtelling; that is, bringing to light the Word of God and its meaning for the current generation and cultural context you find yourself in.

Serving—This gift is also called the gift of "helps." Serving is the ability to demonstrate love by meeting the practical needs of others. This is derived from the same Greek word that we get the term "deacon." It is often demonstrated in the church by communion stewards, ushers, hostesses, nursery attendants, food and clothing pantry workers, shut-in ministries, ministries to the handicapped, and the like. See Acts 6:1-4 in regards to this gift.

Teaching—This is the ability to study and explain God's Word to others in a clear, interesting, and edifying manner. It is intended to help bring believers to a deeper maturity in Christ. Examples of this include: disciple-makers, classroom teachers, Bible study teachers, and teaching/Christian education pastors. 1 Timothy 4:16 (as well as the rest of the book) would be a good place to begin in looking into this gift. This verse also outlines the importance for teachers to pay close attention to what it is that they are teaching for it ensures salvation for both themselves and those they teach.

Encouraging—This gift is also commonly called "exhorting." This is the ability to strengthen or lift up others through personal counsel. This is also the ability to inspire others to action, awaken renewed spiritual interest, or steady those who are discouraged or faltering.

Contributing—This is also simply called "giving." This is the ability to earn and give money or things for the advancement of God's work or meeting individual needs. Again, I fully recommend picking up and reading Dave Ramsey's works whether you feel that you have this gift or not. But, if you do, it will be especially blissful for you. As a reminder, this does not have to do with the "tithe." All Christians, Biblically, are commanded to tithe. Giving is the spiritual gift to go above and beyond. For example, my dear friend Jeff has this spiritual gift. When he sees someone in need, he can't stop himself from doing something about it. God has wired him in this way and blessed him to be able to enter this giftedness. I (though

I love giving) do not have this as a primary spiritual gift, but I am still called to tithe[138].

Leadership—In the Greek, leadership literally means "the one who stands in front." This is the ability to lead in matters of church organization and government. Leadership is to direct and organize the larger group of believers so that each one is released to perform his or her ministry without the obstacle of disorganization. If you feel that this gift is even slightly in your personal gift mix, I recommend that your third step in your discipleship journey be in reading through the works of leadership experts, such as Dr. John Maxwell, Bill Hybels, Dr. Henry Cloud, Andy Stanley, and others.

It would be good to point out that Biblical leadership is actually all about being the lead follower. You're not leading people to follow you. You're leading people to follow Christ. Implied in this is that you're following Christ with reckless abandon yourself. If you're not following first, you're not really leading. You're just trying to get a group of people to worship you. Followership precedes true leadership and is a key to Godly leadership.

Mercy—Mercy is the ability to empathize with those in distress and provide comfort to them in a way that goes beyond normal Christian concern. For this person, you would look at the story of the Good Samaritan in the Bible, as well as the life of Mother Theresa. This is the gift of caring. Someone who has the gift of mercy may not have the ability to give financially to a person in need, but they'll give them the shirt off their back and all of their lunch money without thinking twice. This is also the person you automatically go

---

[138] If you've ever wondered if pastors tithe, the answer is yes. At least, any pastor following their own advice tithes. I'm told that Rick Warren, author of *The Purpose Driven Life*, actually reverse-tithes. That is, he tithes 90% of his paycheck back to God. That is the gift of giving in action in a great pastoral example!

to when rough times occur, because they'll not only listen to you, they'll enter your pain with you and help you bear it.

This list is not extensive. Certainly others will wish to look into the gifts of administration, tongues, interpretation, and several more. Very likely one or more of the spiritual gifts tests you took may have had an explanation of your gift, as well as many places you can find them shown or explained in the Bible. Knowing your spiritual gifts is an important aspect of furthering your discipleship journey. God has equipped you to do something for His kingdom. If you remain ignorant of what that role is, you'll constantly feel a level of spiritual stagnation haunt you. Find what you were (re)born for and your walk with God will explode with joy and a feeling of overwhelming contentment. You'll start to make statements like, "I was made for this." Once you've begun to discover your spiritual giftedness, it is up to you to find ways to use these gifts in your own local church and the Church. If you need help finding something that fits your giftedness, be sure to talk to a pastor at your church and find out where you can plug your giftedness into what God is doing. I promise, you will feel exhilarated if you do.

Just like your faith, these gifts can only grow as you give them away. If you keep them for yourself, they will diminish and even start to fester.

Lesson 10 Assignment Sheet

1. Daily Quiet Time
   a. Daily prayer, reading, and application of God's Word and time with Him.
   b. As you spend time with God this week, take a moment to evaluate your role in the church where God has placed you. What are your areas of giftedness? Where can you best use these gifts in the service of the Gift-Giver? Remember, all of us have been given as a birthright at least one spiritual gift. Your duty is to find it, develop it, and begin to exercise it. How can you serve God with what He has given you?

2. Scripture Memorization
   a. Review 2 Corinthians 5:17, 1 John 4:8, Revelation 4:8b, John 15:7-8, Psalm 119:11, Psalm 119:105, 1 John 5:11-12, John 16:24, 1 Corinthians 10:13, Proverbs 3:5-6, and John 15:4-5.
   b. Learn Philippians 4:4-5.

3. Prayer Partnership
   a. Continue to grow in your accountability and prayer partnership with another from the group.

4. Quiet Time Log
   a. Turn in this week's QTL to your disciple-maker.
   b. Begin a new QTL for this week.

5. Don't give up!
   a. I know you're learning and retaining quite a bit of Scripture as well as the lessons and your new

challenges. Encourage one another to keep going. You only have two more lessons in this course, and the God who started a good work in you promises to bring it to its fulfillment.

> "Rejoice in the Lord always; again I will say, rejoice! Let your gentle spirit be known to all men. The Lord is near."
>
> Philippians 4:4-5 (NASB)

Lesson 11—

Who is Lord, Anyway?

In his article *My Heart, Christ's Home*, Robert Boyd Munger paints the picture of what it would look like if Jesus were to be accepted into the hallowed walls of our heart in the same manner as our physical house. In this imagery, Munger takes very literally what Jesus says in Revelation 3:20, "Behold, I stand at the door and knock; if anyone hears my voice and opens the door, I will come in to him and eat with him, and he with Me." This beautiful word picture analogy begins with Christ entering our hearts, and going into the "study room".

Munger describes how "the study/library" in our mind is the first room of the "house" Christ is welcomed into. It is, as he paints the image, a small room with thick walls. "In a sense, it is the control room of the house[139]." Here Jesus looks through the books and magazines we keep lying around in our mind. "As I followed His gaze, I became very uncomfortable...there were some books on the shelves His eyes were too pure to look at. On the table a few magazines a Christian has no business reading[140]." In humble submission, Munger's spirit turns to Jesus and asks for His help to clean up this room.

---

[139] Munger, Robert Boyd. *My Heart—Christ's Home*, IVP Books: Downers Grove, IL, 2001, 11.

[140] Ibid.

From there, Jesus is invited into the dining room. This is "the room of appetites and desires." Here, Jesus sits down and simply asks, "What's on the menu?" Munger's spirit replies, "My favorite dishes: money, academic degrees, [and] stocks, with newspaper articles of fame and fortune as side dishes." Though there was nothing inherently bad in each of these things, they did not seem to satisfy the Savior. Jesus' plates were served, though, saying nothing, He did not eat. Looking back at Munger's spirit, Jesus said, "If you want food that really satisfies you, do the will of your Heavenly Father[141]."

From the dining room, we are swept away to the living room. In this room a quiet and comfortable atmosphere is found, along with overstuffed chairs, a fireplace, and comfortable sofas. Here, Munger's spirit meets with Christ and morning after morning, it is taught by Him. Unfortunately, after some days of rush, he comes down the "stairs" and notices that Christ has been waiting patiently for him to show up to no avail. Here Christ reveals to him that He desires intimate daily time together, not just for his spiritual enlightenment, but because Christ genuinely wants it as well.

As the story moves on, Christ enters into Munger's workroom, his rec room, his bedroom, and even the hall closet. After reluctantly giving Christ control over each room one by one, finally his spirit comes to the realization that perhaps Christ should not simply be invited into each room of the house, one by one, but should, in fact, simply be given the deed to the entire house. Here Munger's spirit said, "Lord, is there a possibility you would be willing to manage the whole house and operate it for me…" Jesus confidently replies, "I'd love to! This is exactly what I came to do. You can't live the Christian life in your own strength. That is impossible[142]."

---

[141] Ibid., 19.

[142] Ibid., 58.

Munger's spirit joyously replies in a bit of inspiration, "Lord, You have been my guest and I have been trying to play the host. From now on, You are going to be the owner and master of the house. I'm going to be the servant[143]." With that, Munger [144]signs over the deed to his house/heart to Christ. His heart became Christ's home.

This is the imagery we need to have as we begin this lesson. In it, we will talk about the implications of Christ's Lordship in our lives. We will need to confront questions like, "Who is really in charge of my life?," and "Am I really as transformed as I am informed?" Through this lesson, we must also answer the ultimate question of "Are you going to stay in charge of your life, or will you give it over to Christ's ownership and Lordship?"

Take out your own Bible and read through Philippians 2:5-13. Go ahead and read that now. In this section of Scripture, we see that every knee, whether in heaven, on the earth, or under the earth will bow to Christ's Lordship. Therefore, Paul informs us, we are to work out our salvation with fear and trembling. Keep in mind, Paul is not here telling us that we work for our salvation, but through our salvation. The truth of the matter is, we are in a relationship with the God of the Universe when we come to Christ. As we have already uncovered, Jesus the Christ calls us friends, brothers, beloved children, and blessed bride. This is the aspect of God that shows that He is love (recite 1 John 4:8 from memory). But, just as we discussed in lesson two, we cannot forget that Christ is Lord of all. He is holy, holy, holy (recite Revelation 4:8b from memory here)[145].

---

[143] Ibid., 59.

[144] Just curious if you're getting tired of saying the word "Munger" yet in your mind? Munger. Munger.

[145] Were you able to recite those verses from memory? If not, don't beat yourself up. Just reapply the principles you've learned and keep hiding these verses in your heart.

As the holy and sovereign Lord of all, we will bow our knees to Him and, like the angels in Revelation, become broken before His majesty. Remember, we must keep a delicate balance between the love of God and holiness of God. If one or the other is out of balance, then we do not have a proper picture of Who God Is. In the religious life of many millions of people in the thousands of years of Christian history, the holiness of God was often emphasized over the love of God. In today's day and age, however, it is certainly the other way around. This is why T-shirts exist that say "Jesus is my homeboy." We are skewing God's character towards His love and forgetting about His holiness.

We must remember that Jesus is not only our friend and Father, but is the returning King we see in Revelation Who will come to "trod the winepress in His wrath." There needs to be a certain level of reverence in us towards the coming King of Kings. We often live our lives as if this were not the case. In effect, we accept Jesus as Savior, but not as Lord. We call Him friend, but do not also recognize Him as Master. This must come to an end. There's simply far too much Scripture and revelation[146] that shows us that, very simply, every knee will bow.

Notice with me, that something very striking is implied in this verse (and stated more plainly elsewhere) that every single knee of every single person ever to live *will* bow before Christ. This should say something in our lives. You see, we know that not every person will bow his or her knees willingly before the Lord. It doesn't take much of a look around to know that many want nothing to do with Him, while others claim His name and yet truly live and think like those who want nothing to do with Him. In this, not everyone seeks and finds the narrow gate of true salvation in Christ.

Few *truly* call on His Name for salvation. If this is indeed the case, then when every knee bows before Christ, only a fraction will

---

[146] I don't just mean "book of" here.

do so willingly and in humble reverence. God will simply humble others. Jesus said that "He who exalts himself will be humbled, and he who humbles himself will be exalted." I believe this applies also in the "great and glorious" day when we all bow to Christ as Lord, Savior, King, and Father. If this is true, we can take by extension the fact that in our lives today there are people who willingly bow before the Lordship of Christ and others who will wait to be forced to do so on the Day of Judgment.

Which are you? Are you submitting your life to Christ's Lordship? Or, in your own power, are you falsely claiming the name of Jesus while never truly giving your life over to Him as both Savior *and* *Lord*? Master story-teller, Ted Dekker, wrote in his non-fiction work, *The Slumber of Christianity*, that "Christians aren't really so different from non-Christians, certainly not on the scale you would expect considering the promises of love, joy, and peace boldly pronounced from thousands of pulpits across the land. We spend our money on the same kinds of entertainment, we buy the same kinds of food and clothes, and we spend as much time searching for purpose[147]."

Ask yourself honestly if this describes you? Do you recognize Christ as Savior but do not reverence Him as Lord? In his work, *On Tiptoe with Joy*, Dr. J. T. Seamands says, "Christ may be Savior, but not sovereign—living in our hearts, but not completely ruling our lives...He lives in our hearts as resident, but not as president[148]." Echoing this thought, Dr. Bill Bright wrote in *How You Can Be Filled with the Holy Spirit*, "We cannot control ourselves and be controlled by the Holy Spirit at the same time. Christ cannot be in control as long as we are on the throne. As an expression of our will,

---

[147] Dekker, Ted. *The Slumber of Christianity*, Thomas Nelson: Nashville, TN, 2005, 9.

[148] Seamands, John T. *On Tiptoe with Joy*, Baker House: Ada, MI, 1973.

we must surrender the throne of our lives and begin drawing on His resources to live a holy and fruitful life.[149]"

Read back through the quotes above. On a separate sheet of paper, write your response to each one. How do these apply to you? What is God saying to you through them? What are you going to do about it?

There are a few places in Scripture that shock me every single time I read them. Perhaps the foremost of these is Matthew 7:21, where Jesus says that "Not everyone who says to Me, 'Lord, Lord' will enter the kingdom of heaven, but only he who does the will of My Father Who is in heaven." This alone should show us that the issue of the Lordship of Christ is a huge stinkin' deal[150], and a large aspect of true discipleship. 1 Peter 3:15 gives us the clear command, "But in your hearts set apart Christ as Lord."

Jesus doesn't want to be a resident in our lives; He wants to be President. He doesn't want to be a guest in our hearts; He wants us to turn over the deed. This is the difference between someone who comes to Christ and says only with their mouths, "Lord, Lord," and the person who has actually given Christ Lordship of their life. Notice, the only one who enters the Kingdom of Heaven is the person who has truly given Christ Lordship and done His Father's will.

For a moment, let's take a look at the God-of-Love side of this. Turn in your own Bible to John 13:1-20 and read it now before continuing. Notice the striking picture of love portrayed here. Jesus, who is the Creator and Designer of everything from the atom to the farthest galaxy from us, bent down on His hands and knees and washed the disciple's feet. The true impact of this may be lost

---

[149] Bright, Bill. *How You Can Be Filled with the Holy Spirit*, New Life Pubns, Peachtree City, GA, 2002.

[150] Which is, of course, the cousin of the big hairy deal you drew earlier. Feel free to doodle again if you want to.

in our cultural setting. Back in Jesus' day, people traveled from town to town on Roman roads. As a result, many different types of working beasts were moved across these roads. These were the same roads travelers would use. There were no cars. This wasn't even the Oregon Trail[151]. People would more than likely step in whatever was caked on the roads. On top of that, there was no such thing as a tennis shoe. They wore sandals that were mostly open and made of thin leather.

Imagine again what you read in John 13. Jesus bent down and likely wiped dried mud, poop, and who knows what else off the disciple's feet. He then told us that if He were to be Lord of our lives, we would have to allow Him to do this to us, and that we would have to do this to others. As disciples, He called us to follow His example. This speaks volumes to what we're talking about here.

So what does this have to do with where we are right now, and our personal lives? Dr. Charles Lake teaches that the true Lordship of Jesus Christ implies at least three things. First of all, it implies absolute ownership. We belong to God alone. We are His possessions. If we are to be true disciples of Christ and hear Him say, "Well done, good and faithful servant," then we must recognize that we belong fully to God. We are not our own, we have been bought with a price, as Paul says in 1 Corinthians. This truth should impact the way we live our lives from the most very foundational places of our being.

The second implication found in Christ's Lordship is His sovereignty. Not only is Jesus our friend, He is our Ruler and our King. Though Christ Himself calls us friends and brings us up to a level we could never achieve on our own through any effort, this doesn't change the fact that Christ is eternally and immeasurably

---

[151] If it were the Oregon Trail, everyone would have died of dysentery. At least, that's what childhood memories of playing that game would lead me to believe.

higher than us[152]. We are not equal to God. We cannot become as He is. No amount of effort can produce this. We must bow to Him, and not ourselves or manmade creations, as Lord.

The third thing the Lordship of Christ implies is unlimited power. The God called Trinity is the only source of our strength in all things. Jesus asked us to drink of Him and eat His flesh. He told the woman at the well that if she would simply have recognized Him for what and Who He is, He would have given her streams of living water that could quench her eternally. Christ is the source of our life. His Lordship implies that we are receiving our life from Him; we do not (and should not, though we try) live our lives in our own power.

In my "free time," I work as a staff writer for IndieVisionMusic. com. Through that role, I get to meet some amazing people. A couple months ago, I had the opportunity to do a phone interview with Brian "Head" Welch. When I was a teenager, "Head" was a founding member of the band KoRn and was living the rock star life to the fullest. A few years ago, however, he turned his life over to Christ. Because Christ was now his Lord (as well as his Savior), he had to give up living for himself.

His story is actually pretty amazing. When I interviewed "Head" about his new band, Love and Death, Christ shined through everything he said. You could hear the joy he had found in Christ. That joy came from the fact that he was once living whole hog for himself, but was completely empty. He had everything the world could offer in money, fame, and self-gratification, and yet something was missing. When "Head" came to Christ, he didn't just dip his

---

[152] Most people seem to think they'll get to heaven with a "Jesus is my Homeboy" attitude. In reality, every time someone met God in the Bible, they fell on their faces and trembled uncontrollably. This is another reason it was so shocking for Jesus to call us "friends."

foot in the water, he dove in headfirst[153]. So deeply had Brian come to understand Christ's Lordship that during a special feature he wrote for our site he stated, "Like fish move and exist in water, this (Acts 17:28) is saying that we all live, move, and exist in God. He is in us, and all around us. We can't breathe without Him." Talking about John 14:21, "Head" went on to say,

> Jesus Christ, you know that guy they call the Son of God that people have been talking about for centuries? This says He will actually appear to anyone who gives up everything to know Him—friends, jobs, or whatever He asks you to give up (maybe not visually appear to you, but in one way or another to where you know for sure it's Him). The cool thing is, He just wants to see if you'll obey Him, because He gives you the people/things back later on, or gives you better people/things[154].

"Head" gave up everything to make Christ his Lord, even though he had a lot to give up. So, we must now ask ourselves, is Jesus really Lord of my life? Is He Lord without question? Is there any room in your heart, following the analogy from Munger, which is not yet ready for Christ to occupy and own? What are the rooms or "hall closets" that you are hiding your deepest fears, sins, regrets, and pride from Christ that you will not allow Him to open? Now, be brutally honest[155], who holds the deed to your spiritual house? Answer these on another piece of paper, or journal them. Take some serious time to think through this matter.

---

[153] See what I did there?

[154] Check out www.indievisionmusic.com for this and many other interviews I've had the blessing from God to be a part of. [Geesh, Shameless self promotion, much?]

[155] As in, deepest darkest secrets level of honesty…

If Christ truly is to be Lord, then how does the Lordship of Christ affect our daily lives? Let's look at several areas of life that are common to us, yet also commonly overlooked in this regard. First, let's look at your job or vocation. What does the Lordship of Christ mean for this? Does your job glorify God? Are you using your job to accomplish His purposes? Are you a witness to those around you? Merely statistically, you spend more time at work than you do (very likely) at home, with your kids, and/or doing the things you love in leisure. If this is true, the issue of Jesus' Lordship will hit very hard here.

Ask yourself; does my job glorify God? Most vocations are neutral in this regard. They are what you make of them. There is no such thing as a job waiting tables that does or does not glorify God automatically; it's what you do while at that job that becomes the variable. You have to ask yourself what you're making of what God has given you, and if, like the Bible says, you are working that job as if you worked for Christ directly. In some cases, however, you may work in an industry that can very clearly glorify God, or attempt to remove glory from Him.

Whereas most jobs are spiritually neutral, some are clearly against God's will and Word. You cannot, in my estimation, work at a strip club and claim that you're doing it to glorify Christ as Lord of your life. Neither can you work in the porn industry and claim the Lordship of Christ in that. While those are extreme examples, there are several industries that set themselves against Christ. In this, you have to ask yourself, "How is this showing Christ as Lord in my life?" For a great example of how Christ's Lordship can be an agent of change in such an industry, however, check out xxxchurch.com.

Next, we come back to material possessions and wealth. Far from the false prophets of our age that tell us that if we are truly in the Lordship of Christ then we will be rich and have health and our every desire, Christ tells us that if we are to follow Him, we must sell our junk and give the money to the poor. In the book *Radical*, David

Platt shows us that this charge from Christ may not mean that we must certainly sell everything we have, but it certainly shows us that everything belongs to God. If God reveals to you that your true lord, like the rich young ruler found out, is something you own (which means that it truly owns you) then you must remove that from your life. If your boat, collections, car, TV, or other things are truly lord in your life, and you could not give them up if Christ asked you to, then there is a clear red flag.

I struggle in this area, myself. Though my wife and I set in our budget a bi-weekly personal fund that we can spend on whatever we wish (which is not very much), I find that this fund is often spent on some gadget, album, movie, or video game. When Christ first confronted me about this and showed me that my unspoken desire to be possessed by these materials (for they were truly material possessives in my life) was removing His claim as Lord of my life, I had to come to a radical decision. For one whole year, I didn't allow myself to purchase anything that could be lord of my life (aside from necessary food and clothing).

At first, this year seemed like it was going to be hell on earth for me, because I couldn't spend time with what I had made my lord. The glorious truth, however, was that I found that when Jesus was back on the throne and I was not being possessed by material things, my life was much better. I soon found I didn't need to chart out every band that was releasing an album I wanted. I didn't need to hoard movies for the simple sake of having them. And, while it is great to be well read and have many books, the fact was, I was accumulating several at a time and reading only a small handful. If Christ is truly Lord, how we spend our money and what we allow to possess us should reflect His Lordship.

Next, Christ's Lordship should be reflected in our affections and passions. What we give ourselves over to should match up to what Christ's will is for our lives. We should be passionate about what He is passionate about. In other words, we need to find where our smoke screens are. Why is it that the average Christian broadcast spends most of its time either talking about personal wealth or the End Times, when Jesus spent most of His time tending to the needs around Him and speaking on behalf of the poor? As Mike Azar once pointed out to me, if you were to take out the sections of the Bible that focus on the End of Days and then those sections where the Bible talks about the poor and how we are to love our enemies, you would find that the stacks would not even come close to comparing to one another[156].

If Christ is truly Lord, our hearts should break for what His heart breaks for. This doesn't mean, nor am I implying, that every one of us should or could become the next Mother Theresa. If this is what God has for you, then that is fantastic, but you must also remember how He has gifted *you*. It does imply, however, that Christ's Lordship should affect us to where we're looking for what's on His heart wherever we are and working, through the Spiritual Gifts He's given us, to help. Look around you for whatever pierces Christ's heart, and ask yourself if you truly have any concern for it whatsoever.

For just a moment, allow me to shed light on something that is very much culturally bound to our age, and yet has the potential to be a huge aspect of Christ's Lordship. In today's day and age, we are more shaped by our media choices than ever before. The magazine *Youth Leaders Only* (YLO) suggests that the average teen spends 7.5 hours a day consuming music. The average grown-up may find this number to be a bit smaller, but this will hold less and less true as the current generation ages into adulthood. On top of 7.5 hours of

---

[156] Oh, and just in case, the side with loving enemies and helping the poor would GREATLY dwarf the side about the end times. I've always felt that if we worry about the more important matters, we'll be ready for the end times, as well.

music, we likely spend well over two to three hours a day watching TV, movies, and spending time on the Internet[157].

Just like your job, the media is a neutral tool, to be sure. There exists good and edifying music and there certainly is garbage that will ruin your soul. The problem is, the vast majority of it falls into the latter. Often times, we find ourselves listening to music and watching movies that blatantly go against what God has said we should allow in our minds. Check out the P.E.R.T. P.L.A.N. in Philippians 4:8. Paul teaches us that we should have a filter for what we allow into our minds and souls. That filter can be easily remembered by the acronym P.E.R.T. P.L.A.N., for which I am indebted to Joe Ganahl. Just as Pert shampoo protects our hair, the P.E.R.T. P.L.A.N. shows us how to protect our minds. "Whatever is Pure, Excellent, Right, True, Praiseworthy, Lovely, Admirable, Noble; Dwell on these things" (Paraphrased, Emphasis Joe's).

Just as money is a common god in our culture, the media can and will do its best to defame God, skew your perspective on Him, and even outright lie to you about how life is supposed to be. Most people don't think about this, because the media has done such a good job of hiding its allegiance to the enemy. Again, not all media is wrong, but you cannot claim Christ as Lord and listen to music or watch visual media that openly attacks God, is near-completely sexual in nature (even in jokes), is violent for the sake of violence, or subverts God's Word. Though it is almost completely impossible to filter out all the garbage out there and still consume any media at all, we are required to implement a filter that will help us lessen this in all ways possible if Christ is going to be Lord. There's a great amount of good God-honoring heavy metal, Rap, pop, slam poetry,

---

[157] With the advent of tablets and smartphones, we're often doing two or three of these things at the same time. It's like we're racing to see who can get to the end of the Internet first.

rock, and even easy listening out there (among others)[158]. Musically, there is just no excuse. The same isn't quite as true in movies and TV. However, while it is true that there simply aren't too many good alternatives in terms of T.V. shows and movies, this doesn't excuse us. Healthy alternatives are out there.

You must install a filter into your life and begin to look at what you're consuming. After all, the average Christian spends less than 15 minutes with God a day in prayer and Bible study and over 7.5 hours listening to music and watching movies. Which do you think is influencing you more? I'm not asking you to become Amish, but you must become a priest of the culture and ask yourself, "Who is Lord? Who do I want to be in love with?" If your favorite show glorifies an improper sexuality, attacks the deity of Christ, or goes against God's Word in any number of other ways, it needs to go, no matter how funny it is. Imagine listening to music that called your wife/husband dirty names, portrayed him/her as a tyrant, and influenced everyone to be against him/her. You would fight against that, wouldn't you? But, we allow our media to do the same to Christ, who is truly the Love of our life, and we don't even raise a finger. The Lordship of Christ should affect our media choices.

In addition to these, Christ's Lordship should affect our parenting choices, our spiritual gifts (as discussed previously), our sex life, our physical body, and many other areas. You must take these various areas of your life before Christ and ask Him if He is Lord of all. This can be a terrifying process. It's hard getting rid of the many (mini) gods we've allowed in our lives, but this is absolutely necessary. Christ has spoken clearly about what a godly sex life looks like. He has told us that we should treat our bodies as His temples. We have clear spoken revelation from His Word. We must take our lives to Him and give Him the deed to it all, even if we feel like we're being

[158] Fun with shameless promotion! Be sure to check out www.indievisionmusic. com to find more of these.

"destroyed" in the process. I promise you a greater return for your investment than you could ever imagine.

To close, I will adapt for you "The 7 Marks of a Spiritual Man" that are found in A. W. Tozer's *That Incredible Christian*[159]. If we are to be truly spiritual persons (with Christ as Lord of all), the following characteristics must be present in our lives:

1.   I will desire to be holy rather than happy.

God does care about our happiness and is going to give us good things, however, this does not come first. Our focus is holiness first. This means that we should never say, "God wants me to be happy," as an excuse to do evil things. God cares about our obedience first. Happiness, it may surprise you to find, will come as a result of our obedience, not at the expense of it. God designed life to be lived a certain way; when we live that way, we find that the joy we had been seeking in other things was here all along.

2.   I will desire to see the honor of God advanced through my life even if I must suffer temporary dishonor or loss.

Today's society is a "feelings" centered society. If something doesn't feel right, or causes pain, then we write it off as "wrong for us." Sorry, life doesn't work that way. Christ told us to carry our cross and die to ourselves. We must come to know that we will glorify God even if it hurts our social status, endangers our security, or brings us ridicule. Right actions produce right feelings, not the other way around.

3.   I will desire to carry my own cross.

[159] Tozer, A. W. *That Incredible Christian*, Christian Publications: 1986.

What this means for you will be nuanced to how Christ is acting in your life. Carrying your own cross may mean personal loss. It may mean standing up for what is right in your job, at your school, or in your marriage even when it will cause you pain. Ask Jesus in prayer today what it means for you to carry your cross. Whatever it means in your case, however, we know that Christ used this analogy frequently alongside the command that we must die to ourselves. It is no mistake in translation that Christ says this. There is a certain level of pain or even a form of spiritual violence and warfare that happens when we give our lives over to Christ. Your old sinful nature that was focused on fleshly things must die for your spiritual self to be born.

4.   I will desire to see everything from God's viewpoint.

The closer you are to God, the further you allow Christ to be Lord of all. The more time you spend with Him in prayer and in reading through His Word, the more your viewpoint and worldview will line up with Him. Too often in life, we look through our own lens to see the world and people around us. In this, we see despair. We see people whom we are angry at, or think evilly towards. However, when we strive to see every person, and every situation through the lens of God's eyes, we see something completely different. That person whom we feel is worthless suddenly can be seen as a misguided treasure of God's, someone to whom Christ feels the same love for as He does you. Truly, even the most wicked man around you is one of God's treasures. When you begin to see them this way, your actions toward them will be different...more loving...more Christ-like... even if they continue to hurt and berate you.

5.   I will desire to die right rather than live wrong.

As my childhood comics would say, "'Nuff said."

6. I will desire to see others advance at my own expense.

Christ proclaimed that He, though He had the right to rule with an iron fist, came to be the servant of all and that we should follow His example. In humility, we are to consider others better than ourselves. This doesn't mean that think of ourselves as pond scum, however. The Golden Rule of "treat others as you would be treated" applies here. We are to treat others as we treat our own persons, and consider them more than we think about ourselves. If everyone did this, the world would be a different place. Despite the fact that few actually do this, we must as disciples of Christ.

As a side note, Jesus told us to wash other's feet in John 13. This is both literal and figurative. If you have not gone before someone and washed their feet as Christ did, you cannot know the depth of His actions. We must wash the feet of others literally, from time to time, to humble ourselves and remind us of just what Christ proclaimed. We must also wash other's feet in a figurative sense at all times by serving them as we would serve Christ Himself.

7. I will desire to habitually make eternity judgments rather than time-judgments.

This goes back to lesson one. The urgent will often crowd out the important in our lives. We must look at things through the lens of eternity. Giving up personal pleasure that lasts only a moment will have an eternal impact, when you turn around and serve others. Skipping a meal so someone who is starving can eat will make an eternal difference. When you begin to look at your choices not through the lens of "right now," but through the lens of the "eternal now," things come into a much better perspective. Look through God's eyes, and ask what the eternal significance of your decisions can be.

This is one of the hardest lessons. Few of the other lessons challenge our daily personal lives like the Lordship of Christ does.

Therefore, you may need to take extra time with your disciple-maker to work through this. You may wish to re-read this chapter several times with an open heart. Very likely, something that was said stepped on your true god, and it was blocked out or skimmed over. Go back and really dig into what it means for Christ to be Lord of ALL.

Remember, one day, every knee will bow. You will either find yourself bowing on that day willingly before the love and Lord of your life...or you will bow in shame before a holy God whom you only claimed with your mouth, but never in obedience. This is not a scare tactic to get you to deepen your relationship with Christ; this is simply the way it will be. Will you hear, "Depart from Me, I never knew you," or "well done My good and faithful servant?" The contents of this chapter may inform what you hear in that moment.

Lesson 11 Assignment Sheet

1. Daily Quiet Time
    a. Daily prayer, reading, and application of God's Word.
    b. As you spend time with God this week, spend some time evaluating God's role in your life. Is He RESIDENT or PRESIDENT? Take some time to re-read the lesson where needed. As you evaluate your heart's atmosphere of warmth for the things of God, pray for His guidance and assistance. Ask yourself (for only you and God truly know), "Who is Lord, anyway? Who am I going to be in love with?" Who is on the throne of your life? Is it Christ, or is it yourself, your media, your drink, your sex-drive, etc.? An honest look at your priorities and spending habits will help you determine where you are spiritually, and allow you to go on growing closer to Christ.

2. Scripture Memorization.
    a. Review 2 Corinthians 5:17, 1 John 4:8, Revelation 4:8b, John 15:7-8, Psalm 119:11, Psalm 119:105, 1 John 5:11-12, John 16:24, 1 Corinthians 10:13, Proverbs 3:5-6, and John 15:4-5.
    b. Learn Matthew 7:21.
    c. Spend the next few days mastering those verses that you haven't gotten word for word memorization on, as well as reviewing those that you have "stored in your heart." You've accomplished a lot with this. Congratulations!

3. Prayer Partnership
   a. Talk to your prayer partner about continuing to get together on a regular basis after the group has "formally" ended.

4. Quiet Time Logs
   a. Turn your QTL in to your disciple-maker.

5. Be careful about becoming overwhelmed. We've come a long way, and you may feel beaten down by the many challenges you've taken on in this course. Remember that you are loved by God, and that this is a process. You may find that you are only able to take on so much at a time, but allow God to continue this work in your heart even after you've "completed" this course. Remember, discipleship is a life-long process.

> "Not everyone who says to Me, 'Lord, Lord,' will enter the kingdom of heaven, but he who does the will of My Father who is in heaven will enter."
>
> Matthew 7:21 (NASB)

Lesson 12—

Go!

We've now come to the final lesson in this course. Can you believe how far you've come in the last three months? If you've been dedicated and committed to a new life in Christ (2 Corinthians 5:17), and have been forging a new life-style along the way, then you've made some tremendous strides in a very short time. You've learned over a dozen Scriptures, word for word, by heart. You've begun the process of rebuilding the entire foundation of your spiritual house with a correct view of God. You've learned what it means to serve in a church with your spiritual gifts. You've made Christ both Savior and Lord of your life.

That is an amazing accomplishment. You are well on your way to a life of discipleship, and are now more fully able to call yourself a disciple of the living Christ. In this time, you've moved from sit-in-the-pew Christianity to actively becoming a part of the revolution Christ started and placed in the hands of the original 11 disciples (plus Paul and Matthias), which has already shaped and changed the world. You're nearly ready to join the full-on revolution and continue the life altering, spirit changing work that Jesus Himself gave to us.

Turn in your own Bible to Matthew 28:19-20. Read the final commissioning that Christ gave to us before He left this earth. His plan to change the world and get the saving message of the Gospel out to it was *you*! You are Plan A; there is no Plan B. You are an empowered disciple. How does it feel? You're now on a journey to disciple others, to teach them all that Jesus has shared through His Word, and to baptize others in the name of the Triune God Who is and has always been. That's right. This isn't just your pastor's job, anymore. This is your mission, whether you would otherwise choose to take it or not.

We are just about at the end of our time together (in group and in this work). However, before your disciple-maker prays a prayer of invocation and commissioning over you, there is yet one last lesson that must be tackled. This is a longer lesson than many, but it is absolutely critical to your commissioning. We must still learn what it means to "GO!" The purpose of this final lesson, then, is to review what Jesus' plan for changing the world is (discipleship) and to take the negative focus away from God's commands and "Thou shalt/shalt not's."

For eleven weeks now, you've shared your life with this process and a group of fellow disciples. So to begin, I want you to reflect and think through what elements have changed your life that were or were not on the lesson plan. There was likely something that you learned from others in the group, or in one (or several) of the lessons that has fundamentally changed who you will be from now on with Christ. Go ahead and write them down in your journal or on another sheet of paper. Perhaps you learned something from your disciple-maker that you notice now and were not even aware of. Be sure to discuss these in your group. This will help to get you ready for this final lesson and possibly serve as a review to help solidify your commitments in this final week.

Overall, this lesson is pretty straightforward. Once you get through the information side of it, you'll want to spend some time talking through this with your group. Be sure to focus on how you can apply (transformation) this to your life. If there's time (or you decide to continue meeting), you may wish to go back through and test to see where you have and have not applied the information in this course to your life. Remember, discipleship is application of Biblical principles into your daily life. Also, never forget that Matthew 28:19-20 not only charges us to GO!, but also reminds us that Jesus is with us to the end of the age!

So now we come to the final question in this course, "If I am discipled, how then should I live?" The Bible has an amazing way of summing this up. Love. But, what does love-in-action look like? The ancient Hebrew people lived their lives by a selection of the Torah (Hebrew Bible/Old Testament) we call the She'ma[160]. The She'ma can be found in Deuteronomy 6:4 and following. Be sure to read this now from your own Bible. Read until at least the start of chapter 7, though you may choose to read further.

The She'ma teaches at least four huge lessons. First of all, it teaches us that we are to know God for who He really is (Deuteronomy 6:4). This was the basis of Lesson 2 in this work. Secondly, it teaches us that we must put God first in our lives (Deuteronomy 6:5). This was the basis of the previous lesson. Third, it teaches us that we must internalize God's Word (Deuteronomy 6:6). This is why we have diligently worked to store the memory verses that can be found at the end of each chapter, word perfect. Finally (though certainly not the fullness of the depth the She'ma holds), we are told to teach God's Word and commands to others (Deuteronomy 6:7).

This last aspect of the She'ma is what the rest of this lesson will focus on. In it, we examine the focal point of the Old Testament, the Ten Commandments, and the focal point of the New Testament, The Great Commandment. First, we will examine the Decalogue (which means "Ten Words", or "Ten Commandments"). If you can do so before we start diving into them, take a separate sheet of

---

[160] She'ma is Hebrew for "hear," as in the start of the phrase, "Hear O' Israel, the Lord Your God is One..." See, even the She'ma is concerned with Who God really is!

paper and try to recite all of the Ten Commandments from memory. Somewhat of a difficult task in today's world, it seems[161].

The Ten Commandments are:

1. You shall have no other gods before Me
2. You shall not make for yourselves an idol
3. You shall not take the name of the Lord your God in vain
4. Remember the Sabbath day to keep it holy
5. Honor your father and mother
6. Do not murder
7. Do not commit adultery
8. Do not steal
9. Do not bear false witness against your neighbor
10. Do not covet

These can all be found in Exodus 20:1-17. I suggest you read them from your own Bible now before continuing on. To be more than honest, we typically look at this as simply a list of don'ts and they seem to produce a negative feeling in our hearts because of it. They don't inspire us to action, but become passive rules we must watch out for. Too many people have been told all their lives that these are simply the lines in the sand that we are not to cross. This is only half the truth. Certainly, we are not supposed to do these things. However, just as Jesus expanded and re-explained many of them (which we will look at shortly), there may exist another side of these commands.

David W. Gill, in his book *Doing Right*, says that there is a relational element or "other side" implied in each of the 10

---

[161] It's interesting to note that we, as Christians, fight and claw to keep the Ten Commandments posted in front of buildings, but can't even remember all ten of them when asked! One should precede the other.

Commandments[162]. Some people see this as the "positive side." Others see that there is a "do this" behind every "thou shalt not." So, let's go through each of the Ten Words briefly and see what the other sides of the Commands looks like[163].

The First Commandment is that we shall have no other gods before the one true God. This is an indictment to protect and prioritize our relationship with God. Certainly, this has been a large focus in this class. Not only is this saying "do not allow things to come between you and God in your relationship," but it is also giving a charge to seek out and remove those things that keep God from being first in your life. If we were to restate this Commandment in a "positive" way, it may sound like, "Do…protect your relationship with God."

The Second Commandment states "you shall not make for yourself an idol." Ironically, this is exactly what the Hebrews did, in the form of a golden calf, as Moses came back down the mountain with the Commandments in hand. At its heart, this Commandment is a charge to not reduce God to any thing or exalt anything else as god. This is a charge not only to remove whatever is in our hearts that's sitting on God's throne (as we talked about with our media choices), but also to actively protect God's rightful place in our lives[164]. It means that we get to know God for Who He is, and protect that relationship as a lover protects the object of his affection. If we were to state this another way, we would say, "Do…get to know God for Who He Is, and worship Him alone, never 'images' of Him or other things."

---

[162] Gill, David W. *Doing Right: Practicing Ethical Principles,* IVP Books: Downers Grove, IL, 2004.

[163] I am indebted to Dr. Wendell Sutton for first introducing me to this concept.

[164] I cannot more highly recommend Kyle Idleman's *Gods at War* for more on this topic. Read it as soon as you can.

The Third Commandment is, "You shall not take the Name of God in vain." This contains within it the fact that we are never to use God's Name as a curse word, nor are we to use it flippantly. It was due to this commandment that the ancient Hebrew people wouldn't even write the Name of the Lord. They would only speak it in absolute reverence. We don't even come close to doing this in our culture. To honor this Commandment, we cannot just stop at preventing God's Name from being used as foul language[165]. We are to make sure we keep a certain reverence about it at all times. It is holy. Remember, however, that the word we use for "name" also implies character. We must protect the character of God in our teaching, our speech, and our dealing with the world.

This Commandment also teaches subtly something explained in more detail in the book of James. It teaches us that speech is a power given to man by God (see also Exodus 4:11-12) that we should not take lightly. Proverbs 18:21 says that "death and life are in the power of the tongue." James tells us that if anyone is able to keep his speech under control, he can control his whole body. We need to be conscious of when we're speaking life or speaking death. Literally, the power to create has been passed to us by God through our speech. Just as God created all we see in reality with words, we're able to create worlds into being with our words. If a person is told enough times that they're ugly, then that reality has been created in them through words. Say it enough times and a person will eventually believe it. To reiterate, our words can create worlds. We are to use our speech as holy and we're especially asked to honor God's name with it. If stated another way, this Commandment may sound like, "Do...actively use your words to honor God's Name, His Character, and speak life over creation."

The Fourth Commandment is that of remembering the Sabbath as a holy day. In today's world, it's nearly impossible for most people

---

[165] Which may even include using OMG in speech and text.

to simply stop. We often feel like we're in charge of the world and must keep moving for it to be sustained. This is far from the truth. While we're never called to be lazy, we are called to find our rest in God regularly. God Himself took a day to rest. If anyone had the power to keep going without rest and gotten away with it, it was and is Him.

This Commandment challenges us to realize that God is in control and to live life in a balanced manner, which includes regular rest. The American Dream of money, fame, and everything it brings is nothing more than a lie from the devil[166]. We're called to live lives where we seek neither poverty nor riches, but balance and trust in God's provision. If stated another way, this may say, "Do…protect balance in your life and rest. God can handle the world without you for a day."

The Fifth Commandment is to honor your father and mother. Certainly, this is the most challenging Commandment for today's world. As a result of broken families and an overall resurgence of deadly entitlement, we're prone to dishonor our parents by default, often. But God placed our parents over us as those who would watch over our growth and our souls, just as He did with your pastor. Just as we discussed our role to our Pastors, we must obey our parents in the things that they are obeying Christ in, and obey Christ at the expense of our parents when and where they are not. Our ultimate allegiance is to God, even above and beyond our parents. This should not, however, give you permission to dishonor them in any way. It simply is there to say that obedience is given to Christ first, but honor is always given to both Christ and our parents. We are always called to honor them.

This does not simply imply your own parents, however. In this command, we are challenged to consciously choose and do the things that protect and honor families; the structure God intended

---

[166] See David Platt's *Radical* for more on this topic.

for the family, other people's families, and even/especially our own family. After all, Jesus said that this was the first Commandment with a promise. If this Commandment were stated another way, it may say, "Do...actively protect your family and the function/role of families."

The Sixth Commandment is that of "Do not murder." This commandment is straightforward enough in meaning. We are not to take the life of another. I will not here get into the heated discussion of murdering vs. killing. There does seem to be some element to the Scriptures that these may not be the same thing, but that discussion is best sought elsewhere. This Commandment is not just about ending a life. There is also the element of protecting life and adding to the quality of life therein. We should not draw the line at death, but, rather, do those things that protect life. This, as with all the Commandments is a very active thing. As such, this is an indictment not only to cause no harm to others, but also to guard all life. If stated another way, this Commandment may say, "Do...actively protect life."

The Seventh Commandment is the one we are most likely and most commonly guilty of breaking[167]. This is the one that says that we're not to commit adultery. The reason I say we may be breaking it the most in our modern world, is because Jesus explained to us that even looking at another person with lust for them in our hearts is adultery. Think about the magnitude of the implications of that statement. That means porn, dwelling on any sexual thought or taking sexual action towards someone who is not your spouse[168], and may even imply the swimsuit edition of your favorite magazine. This commandment goes so much deeper than just some imaginary

---

[167] (cough) as men... (cough)

[168] "Someone who is not your spouse" means anyone not currently your spouse. If you're not married to them, even if you're engaged, they are not your spouse.

line you cross after you're married in fooling around with another person. It also means doing anything of a sexual nature with any person who is not your spouse currently. That means before, as well as during, marriage.

This is a hard commandment, but the breakdown of this commandment in our world is largely responsible for where we are today. God intended for the family to be the basic structure of society. That means one man and one woman who raise their children together and raise them up in the Lord. When things are not this way, society suffers unimaginable harms. This is why the writer of Hebrews tells us that all must honor the Marriage bed (Hebrews 13:4).

Certainly, this steps on our personal "pleasure." We are in a society that preaches and proclaims loudly through television, music, and water cooler conversations how great it is to seek sinful gratification and expect little to no personal consequence. This is not life as God intended it, however; it is a lie. God intended for us to have so much more. We're called, as you will remember, to die daily to our sinful pleasure. We are people who are called to take up our cross. Sure, this is a very hard area to do so, but the quality of the future of our species relies on it.

This Commandment is not just focused on harming your spouse through cheating, but is a charge to protect marriage and the function of marriage at all personal costs. It is not just "not having sex" with someone who is not your spouse; it is seeking after the heart of purity in your life. This command is an indictment to protect marriage and do things that sanctify all marriages, including but not limited to your own. In short, the Seventh Commandment does have to do with sex, but its focus is on sexual conduct, thoughts, intents, and orientations, that violate, pollute, or break down the covenant between man and woman as God intended. If it were stated another way, this Command may say, "Do...protect the sanctity of all marriages."

I would leave this topic incomplete if I did not address the ever-growing trend towards homosexuality in our post-modern world. As disciples of Christ, we must agree with what the Bible says and not simply what we wish it to mean. As such, I cannot say other than that God's plan for us is man and woman. Homosexuality is called out in several places as a sin in the Bible. There is no way around this without perverting Scripture[169]. However, the Bible also leaves no room for violence and hatred against homosexuals, as too many Christians have fallen into.

Take a moment to read through Romans chapters one and two. In this we see that the natural function that God created was man's desire for woman, and vice versa. However, Paul also goes on to say in this that we are not to judge hatefully because, "Such were some of you." Homosexuality is no different or worse a sin than any other, though we often treat it as such. All sin breaks our covenant with God. All sin breaks the heart of the God Who Is Love, and deserves His holy wrath.

To put it more plainly, the issue of a bent sexuality in this manner is no different than a straight person who seeks sexual partner after sexual partner. There is no difference in that sin and the sin of a man who cheats on his wife, for example. Both are perversions of the gift of sex that God has given us and both break the command to honor the marriage bed. Certainly, we see in Scripture, God's anger against the sin of homosexuality, however He is also crushed by our "straight" perversions of sexuality, as well. All sin is sin before a holy God.

Just as any other sin in our lives, Christ has died for our redemption. We are forgiven of our sins when we honestly and humbly repent of them and give our lives back over to Christ. This area is no different. Certainly, I will have well-meaning Christians

---

[169] For an extremely thorough exegetical look at this topic, pick up Robert Gagnon's *The Bible and Homosexual Practice: Texts and Hermeneutics*.

think that I have not been harsh enough with this. Likewise, I will have homosexuals who may read this who feel that I am hating on them. We must allow Scripture to speak for itself. An honest reading, such as in Romans, shows that homosexuality is a sin, but that God loves and forgives, for "such were some of you." This doesn't mean that we can continue in sin, as Paul clearly points out, but we are not allowed to demonize one particular sin, either.

The Eighth Commandment is simply "Do not steal." Again, this is a rather straightforward command. We're not supposed to take things that don't belong to us. This sounds simple enough, that is, unless you've been on the receiving end of a break-in. A couple years ago, my wife was home sick when a would-be thief attempted to break into our house. He began by trying to pry the bedroom window open. This was the very same room Renae was sleeping in and trying to heal. My wife, thinking the noise was simply our cats playing in the blinds, snuck up on the blinds, opening them very suddenly to scare the cat. The cats were not the only ones who ended up scared. Once the thief realized someone was home, he tried desperately to hide his face and split.

The thief may not have gotten away with any of our stuff, but he did steal a certain measure of my wife's security. You can just imagine the frantic text messages I got while trying to help with communion at the church. For this, the thief certainly stole a measure of my security as well. That may be the core of what theft is. You're not just taking something from someone; you're stealing their security.

This Command, then, is a charge to protect the security of others and become a steward of all of God's stuff. Those who know that God owns everything, find that theft is primarily against God even if it affects others directly. Remember, because it all belongs to God, you can't take what you see fit from others. If stated another way, this Command may say, "Do...protect the property and security of others."

The Ninth Commandment is "Do not bear false witness..." This has both the element of lying and the deeper understanding of not defaming or verbally harming others. It all comes down to truth. This commandment is about honoring the truth in all things and protecting against falsehood said of others. In this, you are protecting the character of God. Jesus said that He is Truth. As Mark Twain is said to have stated, "Speak the truth at all times, it's easier to remember." If worded another way, this Command may say, "Do...actively protect and honor truth, especially towards others."

The Tenth Commandment is "Do not covet." This is a charge to admire the blessings God gives and develop gratitude for what God has given you. Truly, the worst plague humanity has seen in its history is not the black plague or AIDS, but a lack of thankfulness. God has given us immeasurably more than we deserve even in our poorest of circumstances. Just as thankfulness can put your prayers into proper perspective, it can do the same for your outlook on life. When you see just how much God has given you, and sacrificed for you, thankfulness should overcome and outweigh your greed for things you do not have.

Of course, this doesn't often happen. We forget to look at what God has brought us through and focus on the storm ahead, instead. We need to remind ourselves frequently of God's grace to put life into proper perspective. This isn't positive thinking for the sake of positive thinking. It's recognition of Who God is and Who God has been to and for us in our lives. If stated another way, this Commandment may say, "Do...be honestly thankful for all you have."

This may be a new flavor for you of the Old Testament law, but it is the Law, nonetheless. Remember, however, that Jesus chided (got mad at) people for holding to the letter of the law, but missing the spirit behind it. Some people (like the Pharisees) were good at doing things for God, but hurt people. That is not fulfilling the Commandments. When Jesus, Himself, was asked which of these commandments was the greatest of all, Jesus said:

1. Love God most of all (Matthew 22:36-37)
2. Love others (Matthew 22:39-40)
3. Love yourself (Matthew 22:39-40)

Jesus said that every single "do this and don't do that" and every ounce of the Commandments, the law, and the prophets hang on this. The imagery is that of a nail holding up a picture or your coat. Without that nail, the rest of it simply falls to the floor. Jesus summed up the whole of the law and the prophets with the above. Literally he said that everything else boiled down to this. This should show that there is something immeasurably more important in what Jesus is pointing to than anything else we could study.

The Bible is a command to learn to love for what love really is. If you remember nothing else in your discipleship (a tragedy, to be sure), remember this. Jesus reminded us that we must love the Lord our God with all of our hearts, all of our minds, all of our strength, and all our soul. That means obeying Him and doing His will. It also means putting God's desires before our own. No matter how you look at it, that's a lot of love!

You may want to write down, on another sheet of paper, each of those categories (heart, mind, strength, and soul) and assess where you are and where you do not currently love God as He deserves. Then, take a moment to give yourself practical and measurable ways in which you can increase your love. This may mean finally getting rid of that media that is slapping Jesus in the face. It may mean working doubles for a short time to get rid of your debt and thereby, your current master. Whatever it means for you, write that down and commit to doing it in measurable and practical steps.

Jesus didn't simply say to love God, however, and stop there. He said that "the second command," meaning it is not equal to loving God, but is darn close, is to love others. Again, this theme is echoed throughout the Bible. God wants us to love...without prejudice...without racism...without bigotry...without animosity...

without greed…without self-filled pride. To sum up the second most important thing in all of life: Love people. As we've discovered, we need to continue in our path of discipleship to see what love really is. Love in truth. Love in honesty. Love with abandon for yourself. Love until it hurts. Love people. Jesus died for them. He loves people so much it hurts Him. You should too. I should too. We should too.

The final charge in Jesus' words is often the most overlooked; love yourself. Jesus says to love others as you love yourself. You are not excluded from the equation, though you do come third. A healthy disciple is one who loves him/herself and is confident in Who God is through him/her[170]. You must find this confidence. God loves you and died for you. God would have died for you if you were the only one who needed it. God's love for you knows no limits and when you hate what God loves (you) and treat yourself like garbage, you are telling God that He died for junk. It's a lie.

This is not some soft-soap message that you can have the best life you dream of, or a message of heresy that you are somehow equal to God (or able to become like God through effort and adherence to the rules), but plain and simple truth. God loves you. When asked to sum up the Bible as simply as possible, the legendary Billy Graham simply said, "Jesus loves me this I know, for the Bible tells me so." God showers us with crazy love.

God loves you with an earth-shattering love. He deems you worthy of this love.

You are His Disciple.

---

[170] Not in their own abilities.

Disciple Commissioning

This is the end of your formal discipleship group. What do you do from here? The final words spoken by Jesus, as recorded in Matthew 28:19-20, tell us that we are God's only plan for the transformation of this world. There is no Plan B. Jesus put the ball in our hands and ours alone.

As He was raised into heaven on a cloud, surrounded by angels proclaiming His glory, He left us with the following command, which is now our battle cry.

1. Go make disciples!
   a. Go baptize them in the Name of the Father, Son, and Holy Spirit.
   b. Teach them to observe God's commands.
   c. Remind them that God is with us, always.

Now that you've entered into your discipleship journey, you are hereby commissioned to GO! Continue the spiritual practices that you have learned. Continue to grow yourself. Continue to hide God's Word in your heart, and GO! You may still feel like you need further discipleship yourself, but at some point, sooner or later, you're called by God to repeat this process and GO! make disciples. You are the warrior/warrior princess that God is sending into this generation. You are Plan A. There is no Plan B...but never forget that it is God who goes with you every step of the way.

You are hereby commissioned. Go!

"Go therefore and make disciples of all the nations, baptizing them in the Name of the Father and the Son and the Holy Spirit, teaching them to observe all that I commanded you; and lo, I am with you always, even to the end of the age."

Jesus' final words to mankind in Matthew 28:19-20

Afterward

This past Thursday I was at work much later than I usually am. At home, my ten-month-old son sat waiting at the front door for me to come home. My wife tells me that each day, around the same time I usually get home, my son crawls over to the door and says "dada" over and over again. On this particular day, I didn't come home as I was supposed to. For a while, Logan was ok. After an hour or so, I'm told, things started to turn. Logan sat by the door, cried "dada," and then buried his face in the carpet, inconsolable.

How long has it been since you sat waiting for God? How long has it been since you were so excited to see Him that you could hardly contain the joy? Can you remember such a time? What we've begun together in this discipleship process is merely that, the beginning. Discipleship is a life-long process of deepening your relationship with God. The 12 lessons we've gone through, while foundational, are not where your discipleship process ends. There's still work to be done. Where you go next, however, is up to you and where God is leading you.

On top of memorizing a verse a week (your pick from your preferred version this time), keeping up with your daily quiet time, and perhaps even keeping a journal or continuing with the QTL's, you should seek greater wisdom on other areas of your discipleship. The areas in which your spiritual gifts were revealed are a good place to start. A person with the gift of mercy and helps, for example, would probably be incredibly edified to read through the life and work of Mother Theresa, as well as *Radical* by David Platt. A person with the gift of leadership should read through the writings of John Maxwell and Bill Hybels (among others). No matter what your spiritual giftedness looks like, there is a wonderful bevy of resources available. You'll find that if you start studying in your areas of giftedness, those teachings will really come alive for you.

As I have mentioned before, I firmly believe that everyone needs to read through and study the basics of financial health. For me, Dave Ramsey's *The Total Money Makeover* has been the best resource to this end. Regardless of whether the gift of giving was in your gift mix or not, this book (as well as his course *Financial Peace University*) is a crucial next step in your discipleship. You will not regret (though you may hate it at first) the budgeting techniques and debt reduction tools that Dave will give you to get rid of that master called money, "As a gazelle delivers itself out of the hands of the hunter." Check out www.daveramsey.com to find a *Financial Peace University* class that is being offered near you, and to find his best-selling books.

Another area that I feel is crucial to discipleship in today's world is a study on authentic manhood/womanhood. We are created as man and woman each in the image of God; however that image has become marred by the sin of this world. For men, I strongly recommend going through Robert Lewis' course *Men's Fraternity*. This can be found online at www.mensfraternity.com. I also recommend, without hesitation, reading *Wild At Heart* by John Eldredge. These two works can do a great deal to help in restoring the image of God in you as a man.

For women, Stasi Eldredge's *Captivating* is a great place to start. I also recommend that guys read through this, as well, to get a better understanding of the inner workings of the other side of God's image. The same holds true for girls, I recommend that you read through *Wild At Heart* to better understand your man. There are many women's resources available. Just check your local Christian bookseller.

Another area that was mentioned, but could certainly be studied further, is that of the Spiritual means of grace or spiritual disciplines. Here, I fully endorse and recommend Richard J. Foster's *Celebration of Discipline*. This is perhaps the foremost work in this field. Another good one would *be The Spirit of the Disciplines* by Dallas Willard. These will help you to better understand silence, solitude, prayer, fasting, and more.

I further believe all disciples of Christ should continue in an understanding of Who God really is. Here, I most heartily recommend *The Jesus I Never Knew* by Phillip Yancey and *Who is This Man?* by John Ortberg. Other great works include Elton Trueblood's *The Humor Of Christ*, C. S. Lewis' *Mere Christianity* and *God in the Dock*, *Dug Down Deep* by Joshua Harris, *The Challenge of Jesus* by N. T. Wright, *Renovation of the Heart* by Dallas Willard, *Crazy Love* and *Forgotten God* by Francis Chan, and *Walking with God* by John Eldredge. Of course, I would be remiss if I failed to recommend again Dr. Cliff Sanders' *Making Sense Out of Spirituality*.

One final area I recommend that every person continue with is to do a study on how to "properly" read the Bible. David Thompson's masterwork *Bible Study That Works* is my most heartily recommended resource. You may wish to read the source material for that book, *Methodological Bible Study* by Robert Traina later in your walk, as well. These two works will introduce you into the world of Inductive Bible Study, a process that has opened up the Bible for me in ways I could have never imagined. Gordon Fee's *How to Read the Bible for All It's Worth* is another great resource.

For further works on discipleship I recommend *The Cost of Discipleship* by Dietrich Bonhoeffer, *Following Jesus* by N. T. Wright, *The Masterplan of Discipleship* by Robert E. Coleman, *Unchristian* by David Kinnamin, and possibly even *Seizing Your Divine Moment* by Erwin McManus, *The Christian Atheist* by Craig Groeshchel, and *The Best Question Ever* by Andy Stanley. If you are a church leader, I cannot more highly recommend the book *Simple Church,* by Thom Ranier and Eric Geiger.

If leadership is in your gift mix in any way, I most strongly recommend Bill Hybels' *Courageous Leadership.* I also recommend almost anything and everything by John C. Maxwell. Of particular importance, however, are *The 21 Irrefutable Laws of Leadership* and *Failing Forward.* Other leadership "experts" include Andy Stanley, T. D. Jakes, Marcus Buckingham, Ken Blanchard, and Warren Bennis. If you are a leader, then you'll need to know that "leaders are readers," and pick up a few leadership books to read through.

To every disciple, I also recommend reading through the collected non-fiction (and fiction for fun) works of C. S. Lewis, Phillip Yancey, Elton Trueblood, Kyle Idleman, and G. K. Chesterton. Some of the older works in this list may be dated at times, but timeless always. I truly believe that there has not been a great Christian mind in the last 50 years that has not used C. S. Lewis, for example, as inspiration. Such masters can lead us all into a much deeper understanding in so many ways. Lastly, I would like to personally ask every person who reads this to read Kyle Idleman's *Not a Fan* as soon as possible. If you need a reminder of what it looks like to follow Christ, that is it.

There are countless other resources I could recommend. As you can see, this has just been the door to a larger world. It is of the utmost importance that you continue diligently (see lesson 1) in your discipleship path. Remember, you cannot take others where you are not going yourself. If you only allow yourself to be temporarily transformed by the work at hand, then you have done yourself and the Gospel a great injustice. Only through a concentrated effort will you continue on your discipleship path, remember all that you have been challenged by, and grow enough to take others along with you.

You have begun the discipleship journey. The next step is to ensure continual growth and start this growth in others.

Now, Go.

Bible Memory Sheet

Ideas to help you

1. Cut this up and make flash cards
2. Hang it in your bathroom by your mirror or across from where you sit.

"Therefore, if anyone is in Christ, he is a new creation. The old has passed away; behold the new has come."
II Corinthians 5:17 (ESV)

"Until now you have asked nothing in My name. Ask, and you will receive, that your joy may be full."
John 16:24 (ESV)

"The one who does not love does not know God, for God is love."
1 John 4:8 (NASB)

"Holy, holy, holy is the Lord God the Almighty, Who was and Who is and Who is to come."
Revelation 4:8b (NASB/ESV)

"No temptation has overtaken you that is not common to man. God is faithful, and He will not let you be tempted beyond your ability, but with the temptation He will also provide the way of escape, that you may be able to endure it."
1 Corinthians 10:13 (ESV)

"If you abide in Me, and My words abide in you, ask whatever you wish, and it will be done for you. My Father is glorified by this, that you bear much fruit, and so prove to be my disciples."
John 15:7-8 (NASB)

"I have stored up Your word in my heart, that I might not sin against You."
Psalm 119:11 (ESV)

"Your word is a lamp to my feet and a light to my path."
Psalm 119:105 (ESV/NASB)

"And the testimony is this, that God has given us eternal life, and this life is in His Son. He who has the Son has the life; he who does not have the Son of God does not have the life."
1 John 5:11-12 (NASB)

"Trust in the Lord with all your heart and do not lean on your own understanding. In all your ways acknowledge Him, and He will make your paths straight."
Proverbs 3:5-6 (NASB)

"Abide in Me, and I in you. As the branch cannot bear fruit of itself unless it abides in the vine, so neither can you unless you abide in Me. I am the vine, you are the branches; he who abides in Me and I in him, he bears much fruit, for apart from Me you can do nothing."
John 15:4-5 (NASB)

"Rejoice in the Lord always; again I will say, rejoice! Let your gentle spirit be known to all men. The Lord is near."
Philippians 4:4-5 (NASB)

"Not everyone who says to Me, 'Lord, Lord,' will enter the kingdom of heaven, but he who does the will of My Father who is in heaven will enter."
Matthew 7:21 (NASB)

Quiet Time Log

Discipleship report for:			Week of:		
Day of the week:	Scripture text:	Study time:	Time up/time to Bed:	Exercise:
Verse: Insight: Application:				
Day of the week:	Scripture text:	Study time:	Time up/time to Bed:	Exercise:
Verse: Insight: Application:				
Day of the week:	Scripture text:	Study time:	Time up/time to Bed:	Exercise:
Verse: Insight: Application:				

Day of the week:	Scripture text:	Study time:	Time up/time to Bed:	Exercise:

Verse:

Insight:

Application:

Day of the week:	Scripture text:	Study time:	Time up/time to Bed:	Exercise:

Verse:

Insight:

Application:

Day of the week:	Scripture text:	Study time:	Time up/time to Bed:	Exercise:

Verse:

Insight:

Application:

Day of the week:	Scripture text:	Study time:	Time up/time to Bed:	Exercise:

Verse:

Insight:

Application:

Prayed with prayer partner?

Memorized scripture? (write it here):

Highlights of the week:

Disciple-maker's comments:

CPSIA information can be obtained at www.ICGtesting.com
Printed in the USA
LVOW12s1349060813

346393LV00001B/102/P